The

WARWICKSHIRE
Village Book

THE VILLAGES OF BRITAIN SERIES

Other counties in the series include:

A list of the volumes currently available can be obtained
by writing to the publisher.

The

WARWICKSHIRE
Village Book

Compiled by the Warwickshire Federation of
Women's Institutes from notes and illustrations sent
by Institutes in the County

Published jointly by
Countryside Books, Newbury
and the WFWI, Leamington Spa

COUNTRYSIDE BOOKS
3 Catherine Road
Newbury, Berkshire

To view our complete range of books,
please visit us at
www.countrysidebooks.co.uk

ISBN 1 85306 652 4

Front cover photo of Aston Cantlow taken by Bill Meadows
and back cover photo of Leek Wootton taken by Miss J. Wardle of
Warwick W.I.

Produced through MRM Associates Ltd., Reading
Printed by J. W. Arrowsmith Ltd., Bristol

❦ FOREWORD

Welcome to the revised edition of *The Warwickshire Village Book*.

The county sits in the heart of England, stretching from Oxfordshire in the south to its northern boundary with Staffordshire.

Warwickshire's history is extensive and varied; it has been ravaged by the Saxons and, of course, witnessed the first major engagement of the Civil War at Edgehill in 1642.

Running through the county we have the River Avon which meanders slowly along a broad, well pastured valley and through the Forest of Arden.

There are excellent examples of castles such as one of England's foremost tourist attractions at Warwick, together with the fine country houses of Baddesley Clinton, Charlecote Park and Ragley Hall, to name but a few.

William Shakespeare is perhaps the most well known literary character giving Stratford-upon-Avon its own special place among the guidebooks. Yet we also have George Eliot, the novelist, and Joseph Arch, who founded the first trade union for farm workers.

This book captures a number of villages within Warwickshire with their history and events. Thanks go to all the W.I.s who have contributed to this book and we hope you enjoy reading it.

Jeryl Stone
Federation Chairman

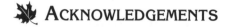 # ACKNOWLEDGEMENTS

The Warwickshire Federation of Women's Institutes would like to thank all those members and their W.I.s who have worked on the research and provision of information and drawings for their villages.

Also a special thank you to Anne Allen, co-ordinator for the project.

County of WARWICKSHIRE

Alderminster Church

🍁 ALDERMINSTER

Standing astride the busy A3400 Stratford–Oxford road, Alderminster must be a familiar sight to the many travellers who pass through at speed.

The church was founded by a community of monks led by St Aegis and sent from Glastonbury in AD 530. After his death in 582 his shrine was a place of pilgrimage until suppressed by the Archbishop of Canterbury in 673. The community was taken over by Malmesbury Abbey, then Pershore Abbey who made it a house 'for maintenance of hospitality and for infirm monks'. At the same time an extension was made for a parish church of the Holy Cross and High Altar of St Mary Minster-Chancel, dedicated on 14th July 1286 by the Lord Bishop of Worcester.

The main part of the village was then at the top of the hill to the north-east, but in 1348 the Black Death wiped out most of the inhabitants, and those remaining grouped their homes near the church.

During the Civil War in 1642 Cromwellian troops were stationed in the village before the Battle of Edgehill. While renovation was going on in one of the older houses a walled-up body was found wearing a Roundhead breastplate.

In 1823 it was decided to build a tramway between Stratford-upon-Avon and Moreton-in-the-Marsh following the main road through Alderminster. A bridge was built over the Avon and the road at Alderminster was straightened so that it only had one track to cross. The day of opening, 5th September 1826, saw a crowd of thousands and celebrations at Moreton.

As there were several hills on the way, and horses were used to pull the tram, a halt was called at the top while the horse was unhitched and placed on the tram. The brake was released and then the whole load careered downhill to the bottom, where normal transport was resumed. The tramway was closed by the GWR in 1869.

During the 1870s a local landowner built 24 houses, the school and schoolhouse in the village. The school, which opened in 1872, was in use until 1971 when due to the retirement of the two teachers it was closed. It is now a private house.

In 1960 about 100 houses were spread along the main road with a garage, post office/store, bakery and The Bell Inn. An ex-army hut was used as a village hall but a new hall was built in 1963.

Since then many new houses have been built and the number of residents has almost doubled. At the same time the post office/stores and bakery have both closed, so villagers must visit Newbold or Stratford for pensions, stamps and food.

🍁 ALVECOTE

Alvecote is a mining village. The mining of coal here in the 19th and 20th centuries has left a legacy of terraced houses, a spoil tip and, when it became flooded due to mining subsidence, the 'Alvecote Pools'. These are now a nature reserve and a Site of Special Scientific Interest, a haven for many uncommon insects, some rare plants and a great many birds.

Alvecote Priory, of which the ruins remain beside the Coventry canal, was a Benedictine priory founded in 1159. Its 14th century remains include a fine moulded doorway and a dovecote. It is now a picnic area.

The priory has an interesting legend attached to it. It was founded by a William Burdett and the legend says that he returned from a pilgrimage to the Holy Land to be told of his wife's infidelity. He killed her in anger, and later, having discovered the tale to be untrue, he founded the priory as a penance.

There is now renewed activity along the Coventry canal with the newly opened marina and an excellent towpath walk.

🍁 ARROW

Nowadays the traffic thunders out of the old Roman town of Alcester on the A422 and rushes off to Evesham and the world beyond and thus you miss Arrow, for the little village straddles this busy highway.

It is an old village, and until recent years was owned by the Marquis of Hertford who still lives in the village at Ragley Hall. Its main inhabitants in those early days were the employees and retired workers from the estate, but the social climate has changed now, and the great estates do not employ a large staff as of old. These days new houses are being built and old ones converted for the folks who commute into nearby towns.

The beautiful fertile land is farmed by the Marquis, and sheep and cattle graze beside woodland alive with deer and pheasant. All around neat hedgerows and well tilled fields give notice of the richness of the land and the careful attention it receives.

On the banks of the river Arrow is an old water mill which, until a few decades ago, was still grinding corn. The original mill was mentioned in the Domesday Book and dates back to 766. The setting is still beautiful and the millwheel still turns, although now it is part of an hotel restaurant.

Upriver from the Mill is Arrow church, a 12th century Norman church which is still lovingly cared for, although the adjacent rectory and coach-house are now private dwellings.

The boundary between Alcester and Arrow is Spittle Brook, and here there is a waterman's cottage and, still in the garden, below the old reservoir, a waterwheel, one of the oldest metal wheels in England, which operated to supply Alcester, 1½ miles away.

Beloved of many generations of children is the 'Elephant' tree! Set in the bank, just beyond the waterman's cottage, is the great trunk of an ancient oak tree which has grown to have all the texture and shape of an elephant. How many childhood fantasies must have been woven to explain his presence there! Sadly, the tree and the waterwheel are both threatened by future development plans.

At the junction between the Worcester and Evesham roads there is a toll house built in the 1850s, which could control both roads and collect tolls for the Marquis from the travellers with their livestock.

On the Worcester Road at this junction lived the wheelwright, and opposite was the forge and the blacksmith's cottage. As the motor car became king the enterprising wheelwright opened a garage, but even this has gone now, and a new house has taken its place. The schoolhouse, which was built in the mid 19th century, and the village shop have both closed, the former being offices.

Ragley Hall, set in rolling parkland, has a commanding position and comes unexpectedly into view in all its grandeur when travelling from Stratford or Worcester. The Hall and park are open to the public, with nature walks and an adventure playground for the children. There is a heronry in Ragley Park, and early mornings will catch a group of herons on the river bank, like old men chatting about the weather.

The Marquis tells this story of the Arrow Ghost. 'There is a spring on the main road between Arrow and Dunnington at the foot of Ragley Park. Towards the end of the 19th century travellers in coaches often saw a little old lady beside the spring begging a lift towards the village of Dunnington. Those who gave her a lift invariably found that she had disappeared when they stopped at Dunnington Crossroad to let her out of the carriage. Eventually someone had the idea of digging around the spring, and they found the bones of an old lady. The bones were reburied in Arrow churchyard in about 1900 and the ghostly old lady was never seen again.'

🍁 ASTON CANTLOW

Aston Cantlow is a village situated seven miles north of Stratford-upon-Avon. The name is derived from the Norman, Cantelupe, which was the name of the baron who built a castle on the outskirts of the village in 1205. Now, sadly, only a few ridges in a field remain near the river Alne. The baron's son, Thomas, born in 1218, became famous as Chancellor of England during the reign of Henry III and following his death in 1282 was canonised by the Pope. Apart from St Augustine, Aston Cantlow is the only parish in England to claim a former vicar as being a saint.

A charter allowing a market to be held in Aston Cantlow was granted to the Lord of the Manor in 1227, and the remains of the market place can still be seen.

The church of St John the Baptist in Aston Cantlow is quite beautiful, parts of which date back to the 13th century. An important event here was in 1557 when William Shakespeare's parents are reputed to have been married in the church. Their first child was also thought to have been baptised here in 1558. Shakespeare's mother, Mary Arden, lived in Wilmcote and his father, John Shakespeare, lived in nearby Snitterfield.

Aston Cantlow today has about 500 inhabitants, earning their living mainly in the neighbouring towns and cities as opposed to earning a living from the land as would have been the case 100 years ago.

Within the parish are the hamlets of Newnham, Shelfield, Little Alne, Billesley and Pathlow which lies on the A3400. Also the former hamlet of Wilmcote which is now a large village.

In 1541 and 1546 blue lias stone from the quarries at Newnham was used to repair Clopton bridge in Stratford-upon-Avon. Billesley was once owned by the Trussells, a family who lived for centuries in Billesley Manor which is now an hotel. The last Trussell was hanged in the time of Queen Elizabeth I as a highwayman. The village itself no longer exists as such, having been destroyed by the ravages of the Black Death in the Middle Ages, the only remains being a few humps in a field near the church of All Saints which is now redundant and closed, opening for only one or two services a year.

Aston Cantlow has a very fine medieval Guild Room opposite the Kings Head Inn. The Guild Hall is believed to have been the home of the Guild of St Mary, first mentioned in 1442, a religious guild which provided priests for the church services. Part of the Guild Hall used to be the village gaol, but the building has now been converted into the village hall. There was a chapel until the 1960s in Chapel Lane with visiting preachers, one of whom was nicknamed 'I be Charlie' because he used to say, 'I be Charlie and I comes from Binton'. Another fascinating character in the history of Aston Cantlow was George Lewing who was the first headmaster of the village school from 1847 until 1873, and left a notebook describing life in the middle of the 19th century. Unfortunately the school in Aston Cantlow was closed down in the 1960s.

In Mill Lane there was a water powered mill, where they produced paper in 1748, needles in the 1800s, and then ball bearings for bicycles. The mill became a brush factory in 1915, but was demolished in the early 1930s.

The railway to Alcester no longer exists in Aston Cantlow but signs of the old track can still be seen, although the site of the original Halt has disappeared.

🍁 AUSTREY

Austrey lies in the northern tip of the county, near junction 11 of the M42, seven miles from Tamworth and eight miles from Ashby-de-la-Zouch. Close by are Twycross Zoo and Market Bosworth, famous for the battle of Bosworth Field in 1485 when Richard III was killed.

Formerly known as Adulfe's Tree or Adulestry (Domesday Book gives Adulvestrev), Austrey had 124 houses and 497 inhabitants in 1841, but only 335 people in 1911. The census of 1981 showed a large increase to 962.

New housing developments are much a part of the village today. Many old cottages were destroyed in the 1950s and 1960s, and only about 40 houses remain that pre-date 1900. Many farms have been sold, land has been absorbed by larger arable farmers and much rich pastureland has been turned to the plough. Several farmhouses have been sold with just a few acres of land.

Nevertheless, throughout the village are many delightful old properties, such as the black and white Bishops Farm, bearing the date 1521. Over the road stands a fine three-storey Manor House. The intriguing Saddler's Cottage stands broadside to Warton Lane, and Farthings is a fine timbered property, once the shop and post office. A modern general store and post office is across the road, providing a wide variety of services.

Built in 1808, the Baptist church stands just off the main road. Many slate headstones are still to be found around the car park. St Nicholas' church looks down over the village, as it has done since the 13th century. The elegant Old Vicarage is no longer the home of the vicar of Austrey and Warton; he now lives in a modern house next door.

Conveniently close to the church is the Bird in Hand pub, the only remaining thatched house in the village. Outside stands a medieval plinth, said to be the meeting place of those seeking work in years gone by. In 1897 a cross was erected on the top of the four octagonal stone steps, to commemorate the Diamond Jubilee of Queen Victoria.

Austrey Parochial School, built in 1850, has been used as a village hall since Austrey Church of England First School was opened elsewhere in the village in 1969. This school is now a primary school, taking children to eleven years old.

As Austrey looks to the future, there are many reminders of the past, like the old Windmill Lane atop of which stood, naturally, a windmill. From here there is a panoramic view over four counties – Leicestershire, Derbyshire, Staffordshire and Warwickshire. Walkers are well catered for. Many bridle paths encourage horse-riding, and the village has several riding establishments in the vicinity. It is also the home of a stable of handsome Shire horses.

Austrey is regularly placed in the Warwickshire Best Kept Village Competition, and came first in 1990 and 1994. Keen gardeners abound, and many open their gardens to the public once a year. There is an active Garden Society, as well as the WI and the Bridge Club. There are cricket and football teams and a Golfing Society. All the organisations support the popular Gala, held every summer on the playing fields. In spite of its being largely a commuter village, there is a lot going on in Austrey.

⁂ BADDESLEY ENSOR

Turn off the A5 Watling Street at Grendon and you are going back in time, for this old turnpike road leads to Coleshill and Baddesley Ensor stands en route up the hill. In 1848, Baddesley's ancient church was pulled down and replaced by the church of St Nicholas. The old pulpit was bought by the Wesleyan Methodists and installed in their chapel. This five-sided black pulpit is claimed to be the one from which Bishop Latimer preached nearly 400 years ago. The same Bishop was burned at the stake by Mary Tudor, saying, 'This day, by God's Grace, we have lit a candle in England which shall never be put out.'

Baddesley seems always to have had a rebel tradition. In 1669, Quakers were considered rebels, and their meetings declared illegal, but they had a secret meeting house in Baddesley. In 1772, when the Quakers were given freedom to worship, Baddesley Quakers built a meeting house of their own. The Quakers used the building until 100 years ago, at which time it was rented to the Wesleyan Methodists. Up until 1931, Quakers from many parts of the Midlands made an annual pilgrimage to Baddesley. The Wesleyan chapel is now no longer used. The Trinity Church stands on Keys Hill, where it was opened in 1863, originally as the Congregational church.

There is a large common adjacent to the Middle School. The school was opened in the 1930s, initially catering for pupils of all ages, but senior pupils now attend school elsewhere. On the last Thursday in July before the school broke up for the holidays, the children would walk in class formation to Merevale Hall where tea would be served to them in the park. After tea, races were organised, after which Lady Dugdale gave and presented the prizes. Finally the Dugdale family would sit and listen to the well-rehearsed songs by the children. For several years the senior girls dressed in white and performed country dancing, accompanied by a teacher on the violin. At the end of the festivities as the children left, they were each given a currant bun and a bag of sugar fondant sweets which cheered them as they wended their way wearily, but happily, home. This event was terminated at the beginning of the Second World War and has never been revived. The First School stands at the end of Maypole Lane in a delightful rural setting.

Baddesley Colliery opened in 1850 and was closed in 1989. It provided employment for many of the male population. Originally it was owned by the Dugdale family of Merevale Hall before being taken over by the National Coal Board. At present, both Baddesley Ensor and Grendon are joining to fight a plan to start open cast mining in the area. The Baddesley rebel tradition still lives on!

🍁 BARFORD

The river Avon meanders through Barford on its way to Wasperton, Charlecote and Stratford-upon-Avon. It is a lively village of undulating fields, cut in half by the noisy A429 with numerous little lanes where new houses stand beside old cottages.

Barford fathered Joseph Arch, who started the National Union of Agricultural Workers in 1872, went to Parliament as a Liberal MP, and who was born and died in the little cottage opposite the church. Every year agricultural workers make a pilgrimage to his grave in the churchyard, and one of the public houses bears his name.

Many inhabitants enjoy a stroll down Church Street, or along the Wellesbourne Road, to do their shopping at the thriving stores-cum-post office, where they can meet acquaintances and have a gossip. The old bakery is now a hairdresser's, and the blacksmith now, alas, practises his art from one of the nearby industrial estates and his forge has been converted into a house. But he and his forebears have left their mark on St Peter's church in the form of the weathervane and wrought iron gates.

The Mill, manufacturing animal feed, goes back many years and the huge lorries turn into and out of Mill Lane several times each day.

St Peter's church has a rector who is responsible also for the parish of Wasperton, a little hamlet a mile along the

Wellesbourne Road, and for Sherbourne, across the river. Sherbourne is more than a hamlet, with a magnificent church, built in the 1860s by a member of the Ryland family. The full peal of bells can be heard joyfully echoing across the water meadows on Friday evenings when bell practice is taking place, and again before service on Sunday mornings.

St Peter's Barford is proud of the fact that it has several times been awarded the coveted prize for Best Kept Churchyard in the diocese, and bears witness to many hours of hard work. The village in a similar competition has won the Best Kept Village award twice.

On the outskirts of the village lies Westham House, an elegant building used during the last war as a girls school, and now as an adult education college. The mellow red brick reflects the sun, and the well-kept gardens are an ideal working place for the many aspiring artists who assemble for painting courses during the summer months.

This is very much tourist country, with Shakespeare and his links a mere 7 miles away. Although not a beautiful village in one sense of the word, all the gardens are bright with flowers and well-tended lawns and the village green, recreation ground and village hall are all neat and tidy. The hall is the memorial to the Lord Lieutenant's father who was killed during the war.

🍁 BARTON-ON-THE-HEATH

Barton-on-the-Heath lies on the crest of a hill just inside the border of south Warwickshire, the name being derived from the word 'barton' meaning homestead. Over the centuries the heathland has been converted to agricultural use and today, of the 33 houses here, two are working farms. It was first recorded in the Domesday Book in 1086 when Robert de Stafford was overlord of Barton manors, and referred to in Shakespeare's *Merry Wives of Windsor*, Shakespeare's cousin Lambert having lived at Leys farm. It is said that Shakespeare walked to Barton, and was refused a loan by his cousin, taking his revenge by writing him into the play as the character Christopher Sly of Barton Heath.

The main part of the village consists of a small triangular green, with a Memorial Well-house in the centre, encircled by several well-kept Cotswold stone houses, a working forge, and the 17th century Barton Manor House. The Manor is a lovely stone built house and parts of it are thought to have been designed by the famous Inigo Jones, for some of the rooms bear the mark of his work.

The old school has closed, and is now well used as a village hall. In the reign of James I, there lived, in the house next to the old school, the lawyer Thomas Dover, the creator of the famous Dover Games which were held annually on Dover's Hill near Chipping Campden. These games, for many years extinct, are now held once more on the same spot as they were centuries ago.

To the west of Barton House stands the church of St Lawrence, a lovely part-Norman building with an unusual saddleback roof. Today the faithful tread the path to worship, as did those in the days of the Tudors who, on passing the rectory, would place food in the wall of the house, for the sustenance of the two priests who lived there, caretakers of the church.

The Old Rectory is a part-Tudor, part-William and Mary building. Part of it was constructed from bricks, kilned only a few hundred yards from the site. Here there lived a lady by the name of Olivia Wilmot, who was married in the church by her uncle, the then rector of St Lawrence's, to J.T. Serres, from whom she later parted. A great mystery surrounds this lady, for she claimed to be the niece of George III and the daughter of the Duke of Cumberland. These facts have never been authenticated, but she was a very talented watercolour artist, becoming a landscape painter to the then Prince of Wales, and to the Court. Early in the 20th century The Old Rectory was a private preparatory school, becoming once more a private home in the 1940s.

Barton no longer has a shop, but is fortunate in having several vans calling with a variety of foods, a regular delivery of milk, a good daily paper delivery, and a fortnightly visit from the library van.

🍁 BEARLEY

Bearley lies just off the A3400 between Henley-in-Arden and Stratford-upon-Avon and is spread over a wooded hillside, with many attractive old farmhouses and cottages and its own shop and post office.

It was first mentioned in the Domesday Book survey of 1086, and was referred to as Byrlei – meaning a fortification in a clearing. At that time it consisted of five 'hides', a hide being an area of land large enough to support a family and its dependants.

There is a local tale associated with Windmill Wood concerning the Miller of Bearley. He is said to return to the woods with six black horses every mid-summer moon to look for his gold, allegedly hidden under two millstones. It is while he is away watering his horses that the youth of the village can attempt to lift the stones and steal the gold!

In 1100 land ownership was held by the monks of Bordesley and a small church was built by them on the hill leading out of the village. Although rebuilt over the centuries some Norman stonework is still visible, including the 15th century font still in use today.

The first known school in the village was set up in the 1820s at No 1 The Yard. This was followed in 1877 by the Board school, built in School Lane, and still standing today in use as a private house. During the Second World War various additional buildings were used as school rooms to accommodate the increasing number of children as the village grew. Finally in 1952 a new infant and junior school was built in Grange Road which was in use until 1988 when it was closed due to falling numbers!

The village still holds the annual village fete in August and on Palm Sunday a procession with palms and donkeys. The opening of the new village hall, an extension of the existing one, will enable villagers to put on entertainment and provide leisure facilities, as well as being a venue for existing village groups.

🍁 BIDFORD-ON-AVON

Bidford-on-Avon, a very friendly larger village, dates back at least to Roman times and Icknield Street passes through the village to cross the river. In 1922 a large Anglo-Saxon burial ground was discovered with a wonderful collection of jewels, shields and other artefacts dating back to AD 500 and more recently further graves were uncovered during excavations for the new car park at the rear of the Anglo Saxon public house.

The river Avon flows through Bidford and during summer months is busy with boats cruising to and from Tewkesbury and Stratford where holidaymakers can join the Stratford canal and so on into Birmingham. It meanders past the Big Meadow where on fine weekends one can see scores of cars belonging to the people who have crossed the medieval seven-arched packhorse bridge to enjoy family picnics. A carnival has been held here for over 50 years with many local organisations benefiting from the proceeds. There is also a safe play area for children, attracting visitors from miles around. There is so much to see, with swans, kingfishers, herons, cormorants, buzzards, moorhens and other wild life, local cricket matches and the pleasure craft at rest at the moorings.

There are some interesting old buildings in the High Street. George Harborne House, a stone and half-timbered building, has been beautifully restored. The Bull's Head was a slaughterhouse nearly 200 years ago, hence its name. The War Memorial records 60 names from the Great War, representing a large percentage of young men who did not return. The Old Falcon Inn, which is now two private dwellings, has had a chequered career having been the pub where William Shakespeare drank, the workhouse, and an antiques centre. Look for the angels on the front of the house facing the church of St Laurence. The church was partly built in the 12th century and the 700 year old tower has a peal of eight bells which are rung regularly at least two to three times every week. It is a large church with beautiful stained-glass windows.

Morris dancing in Bidford has been a tradition dating back

prior to 1886 when it was revived and the Bidford dances were performed outside the Old Falcon Inn. These dances are still kept alive and danced by the Shakespeare Morris Men, especially on Trinity Monday.

Bidford was traditionally an agricultural area and there was plenty of work on the land, also at the brickyard, which has long gone, but there is now a thriving industrial area to compensate, providing work for the locals. One can purchase quality chocolates and confectionery, find home improvements and DIY, have logos printed on sweatshirts and send parcels for delivery all over the country. There are antiques shops, book shops, a French bakery, butcher, and recently a supermarket has been built, all catering for the rising population created by new housing developments.

Residents are served by an excellent Health Centre, providing all amenities, allowing villagers to receive fine medical attention within their own community. The diversion of the A46 allows easy access to Evesham, Stratford-upon-Avon, Birmingham and the M40.

Bidford is striving to move with the times and is a peaceful, relaxed and friendly village which is well worth a visit.

🍁 BILTON

Bilton is a village within the Borough of Rugby. The parish was mentioned in Domesday Book and the name is thought to be derived from Bell, being a stream on which the village stood, and Ton the old English meaning for village.

During the 19th century the village consisted of the church, village green, stocks and ancient cross. There were large estates and some farming land in the vicinity which provided employment for the village people. Now the village is surrounded by built up areas, apart from the south which is still free from development.

As one approaches the village from Rugby, St Mark's church spire stands out. The church was rebuilt about 1350 and is an

Bilton Hall

example of pure Gothic architecture. The late M. H. Bloxham, the celebrated antiquarian, said of St Mark's – 'I have visited upwards of a thousand churches in this country and on the continent but have never been so much impressed as with the grand but quiet beauty of this small village church.'

Closely associated with St Mark's and Bilton village are the Assheton family. They are the patrons of the living and three of the family have served as rectors. As a memorial to his wife Mr Orme Assheton built a Chapel of Ease where services could be held for those unable to walk as far as the church. Nearby, Mr Assheton erected 'The Magnet', a building to be used for social and recreational purposes to attract people away from the public houses. This building has now been converted into cottages, and the road parallel to Main Street is called Magnet Lane. The garden and playground at the corner of Church Walk were given by the Assheton family to the village for all time.

Joseph Addison (1672–1719), a distinguished poet and classical scholar, purchased Bilton Hall close by the church for £8,000 along with the Manor of Bilton. He married the Dowager

Countess of Warwick and they had a daughter, Charlotte. Addison was buried in Westminster Abbey and Charlotte asked to be buried there as well, but as this was not possible she asked to be buried at midnight in St Mark's churchyard. This was carried out but her grave has never been found. Her ghost is said to haunt Bilton Hall.

The Church House is situated near the main road and the village. It serves as a village hall and behind it is the Warwickshire County Council Clinic serving many villages nearby.

Bilton Park was one of the very fine houses near the village and the Prince of Wales, later Edward VIII, played polo here.

Dominating the village green is The George Inn, an old coaching house and a distinctive three storey building. Behind was the village smithy, in use until after the First World War. The village stocks, last used in 1866 stand on the green, as well as a stone cross which may have been a preacher's open air pulpit or more probably a market cross.

Granny's Pie Shop, perhaps the oldest building in the street, has been restored. Its thatched roof has been replaced by tiles from the now demolished Holy Trinity Church in Rugby but the old timbered front has been retained. The main street is lined with a great variety of well stocked shops and there is an air of lively friendliness among the shoppers.

Two Wakes were held in Bilton: Crow Pie and Pindle Wake, the latter in Pindle Field where all the fun of the fair took place including 'catching the greasy pig'. Older residents remember the village as a rural community with cows being driven down the main street to market.

🍁 BINLEY WOODS

The village, unlike most, cannot lay claim to antiquity, for until 1961 the village of Binley Woods did not exist. However, the area has many historical associations, dating back to the Norman Conquest when the woods were 'half a mile long and a furlong broad'. The Cistercian monks of Coombe Abbey held here a Court

Leet with gallows, and an Assize of Bread and Ale.

Situated on the south-east boundary of Coventry and the outskirts of the Borough of Rugby, the community that was to become Binley Woods began its modern development in the 1920s following the sale of the Coombe Abbey estates by the Earl of Craven. During the 1920s and 1930s, people settled in the area, bought land and built homes. In the 1940s they were joined by homeless people from bombed Coventry, who fled to the comparative safety of Binley and lived in shacks, caravans and anything that could be called home.

Some of the original 'pioneering' families still live in the area, and it is they who can recall the days before tarmacadam, when visitors were advised to bring their wellies when they came to call. One elderly resident can remember the days when, if she wanted to go to town, she wore her wellies to the bus stop, left them behind a convenient hedge, and donned her shoes. On her return, the wellies were always waiting for her! Eventually the mud receded and the roads emerged, and the wellies could be consigned to the gardens. Gradually, over the years, residents came to enjoy the 'luxuries' of mains drainage, piped water, and when the old gas lights were considered to be too expensive (at £1.12s.6d per quarter!) they were replaced by electricity.

By the late 1950s the residents were anxious that the area should establish an identity of its own and no longer be confused with the neighbouring suburb of Coventry, known as Binley. Villagers were asked to vote, and the name of Binley Woods was adopted. Since then, the local people have worked hard to create a sense of community.

In 1987, Binley Woods made history when, through a Local Ecumenical Project – the first in Warwickshire – the church in Binley Woods was inaugurated in the form of the village hall.

It is a long time since the woods were 'half a mile long and a furlong broad' but at least the woods are still there. Saved from development through the efforts of a local group, the Friends of Brandon Wood, the village can now boast one of the first Community Woods in Europe, jointly managed by the Forestry Commission and the 'Friends'.

25

🍁 BISHOPS ITCHINGTON

Bishops Itchington lies on the B4551 between Kineton and Southam, two miles from Junction 12 of the M40. The river Itchen meanders to the south of the village and there are panoramic views of the Burton Hills to the west.

The church of St Michael stands on high ground in the village and was built in the year 1872, on the site of the original church of All Saints. The vicar, the Rev. Martin Green retains the traditional link with Bishops Itchington Primary School, which started life in its present form in around 1871 with the amalgamation of the chapel school and the church-run school. There were two chapels in the village, the Congregational built in 1836, now converted into a private dwelling, and the Primitive Methodist which was built in 1856 and today houses the post office and general stores. The village also has a 'chippie', a newsagent, a garage, a local Co-op and a number of thriving businesses including a mushroom farm and aquatic centre, a cattery, and an agricultural chemical firm.

The number of houses in the village is approximately 900, but around the beginning of the 20th century there were only 130 houses. This number increased with the opening of the Greaves, Bull and Lakin Cement Works. The company built homes for their employees and were responsible for the building of the Greaves Club and Memorial Hall; both these institutions are very much in use today. Also popular are the two village pubs, the Malt Shovel and the Butchers Arms. In 1927, in the quarry created by the Cement Works, the fossilised remains of a dinosaur, a 4½ metre long *macroplata teniuceps*, was discovered and is now housed in the Natural History Museum. The Cement Works has been demolished and the site is awaiting redevelopment.

The village originally had a splendid manor house, but it is no longer in its original state having been rebuilt after being destroyed by fire. The wonderful mansion buildings have sadly gone along with the history they held, which included visits from Queen Elizabeth I and Oliver Cromwell.

Life in the village years ago was very different to today.

Washdays were hard work as all the water had to be collected from various wells and pumps in the village and bath night meant a zinc bath on the kitchen floor. Fresh bread was delivered to the door, as was the milk which came by pony and trap and was measured straight from the churn into jugs.

Many years ago the village had its own bus service to Leamington Spa, which was owned by Mr J. Edwards, affectionately known as Jimmy. If Jimmy took 30 passengers to Leamington, he waited for 30 passengers to return to the village. Although offering a different type of bus service there is a Village Taxi operating nowadays which will collect passengers from their houses and drop them at various points in Leamington.

In 1949 the village was unable to form a parish council due to lack of interest from the men. The then President of the WI, Mrs Chapel Hyam, and six other members stood for election together with one solitary man and they were all duly elected. This was highly unusual and attracted much media attention with headlines in the national and local press such as 'The Petticoat Government', 'Seven women may govern Bishops Itchington' and 'The Petticoat Parish goes to the polls'. Today the Bishops Itchington WI still flourishes, the year 2000 marking its 75th anniversary.

🍁 BISHOP'S TACHBROOK

Bishop's Tachbrook, tucked away on a minor road three miles south of both Warwick and Leamington Spa, looks down on the two towns below. Some indication of its age is given by its Saxon name denoting 'the brook that marks the way'. In this instance the brook marked a boundary. 'Bishop's' entered the name after the lordship of the manor was bequeathed to St Chad's in Lichfield and thence passed to the Bishop of Chester.

The origins of the village may be in Oakley Wood. Among the bluebells lie the remains of quite a large fortification which is generally accepted as Roman, but the site has not been excavated and could pre-date the Roman occupation. We know for certain

27

from the Domesday Book that by 1086 there was a flourishing community: the Bishop of Chester held about 850 acres of land; there were two mills, a twelve acre meadow, 27 workers on the land and a priest.

The church of St Chad stands impressively on rising ground. Its earliest architecture is Norman but it has been altered and now contains Perpendicular and Victorian work. The present Victorian font stands opposite a Norman one, retrieved from a neighbouring farm. One window is an early example of work by William Morris and Philip Webb, another commemorates Charles Kingsley's widow, who lived in Grove House on the outskirts of the village. Interesting memorials of prominent families include one to the writer Walter Savage Landor, who as a child delighted in the garden of Savages House, though he sold the property when he inherited it.

The remains of the charming Tudor village can best be seen in the cluster of houses at the foot of the church. These include the fine Bishop's House, The Leopard public house, the old forge and the old inn (now a private house) once supposedly frequented by a highwayman who operated on nearby Fosse Way.

After the Reformation, the Earl of Warwick and other wealthy gentlemen purchased land in the parish to extend their estates. As a result of such purchases the Earl of Warwick became chief landowner and lord of the manor in 1789, until the sale of his estate in the 20th century.

The village school was erected in 1766 on land given by Sir William Bagot at the corner of Oakley Wood Road and Mallory Road. A tablet in the church belfry gives a list of donations ranging from £50 down to 2 guineas – from Sir William, the Earl of Warwick, the then Vicar, members of the Savage family and others. According to a trust deed dated 1771, the actual building was paid for with rents received from some 18½ acres of land leased in the Parish of Sutton Coldfield (Tachbrook was then, of course, in the Diocese of Lichfield, not Coventry as it is today). Whether or not Sir William Bagot owned this land is not clear but certainly it funded the schoolmaster's salary. It is also recorded in a Charity Commissioners' Report in the early 1800s that repairs and a new pump were paid for by the sale of timber felled on this land. At that time there were about 100 children being educated there.

The village population declined in the late 19th century but increased rapidly when it became possible to commute by car to work in nearby towns and cities. No longer was the village a farming community. Red brick took over from timber frames/wattle and daub as the building material – perhaps appropriately in a village that still greets visitors with its Brickyard Cottages.

The original school premises were closed in 1962, a new school having been built on a large area of farmland off Kingsley Road. This now has about 190 children and also a thriving nursery school within the school building. A shield incorporating the arms of the Bagot family hangs in the assembly hall and the children wear a replica on their T-shirts and sweaters. Another link with the past is presented in Tachbrook's own version of a Mummers' Play still performed around the village at Christmas time.

Tachbrook has struggled to maintain its independence from its large neighbour, Leamington Spa. It has managed to keep its school, post office, two small general stores, newsagent and – after a battle – a surgery. The thriving Sports and Social Club is the centre for a wide range of activities and The Leopard is a popular pub and restaurant in the area. The parish provides a site for breeding kennels for the Guide Dogs for the Blind Association.

❦ BOURTON-ON-DUNSMORE & DRAYCOTE

This parish which includes Draycote hamlet, is an ancient one mentioned in Domesday Book 1086 with a population of 150. Today it is around 300.

The parish lies on the southern part of Dunsmore Heath, sloping south to a valley in a tributary of the river Leam. Bourton village is on the higher level (107 metres above sea level) and Draycote in the lower valley (76 metres) – ¾ mile down the hill from the parish church. Although divided by geographical features and neatly separated by a now unused railway line, the two communities have much in common – Church, Parish Council, WI village hall and numerous other groups and activities.

For centuries the land provided the main employment. Before 1939 few men worked outside the parish, the rest were estate and farm workers living in tied houses. The farms remain but the many working horses have vanished, and the farm workers are few.

St Peter's church standing on the edge of the heath is early 13th century. It contains much of interest including a magnificent 13th century font, a parson/clerk pulpit dated 1607, Jacobean altar rails, and it is said, a very friendly ghost in the vestry.

Bourton Hall is a large stone mansion begun in 1791 probably on the site of an earlier house. The earliest recorded landowner was Lewin, a Saxon, who held the manor before the Norman Conquest. It remained with various branches of the family of John Shuckburgh who bought it in 1563, until 1906. Much altered and embellished by the new owner J. F. Shaw, it ceased to be a private home in 1947. After short spells of occupation by Jesuits and a Boys Preparatory School it fell into ruin. In 1979 Ingersoll Engineers bought it for their place of work and restored it to most of its former splendour – a good example of a near derelict house given a new lease of life, to the benefit of the company and the village.

The school was established as a Free School in 1836 for boys and girls, with the building and house attached built in 1847 by John Shuckburgh. It was closed in 1974. Now it, too, has been given a new use as a most attractive guest house.

Between them these three buildings once supplied a great deal of bell ringing. Estate workers for instance, were summoned daily to and from their labours by a bell in the private RC chapel at the Hall. No longer. Even in the church a chiming apparatus is now used. The bells, considered unsafe, were last rung, with some trepidation, for the victory of El Alamein in 1942.

The village hall is an extension of the 'Round House', which was actually octagonal and was probably a toll house with attractive curving architecture, once used as a laundry for the Hall.

One custom remains from earliest times. The parish annually on Martinmas Eve, before sunrise, pays its dues of 1½ pence to the Duke of Buccleuch, Lord of the Manor of Knightlow (Dunsmore is part of that ancient Hundred) at the ceremony of Wroth Silver on Knightlow Hill. If the parish defaults His Grace may demand the forfeiture of a white bull with red nose and ears of the same colour.

Draycote lies between hedgerows, trees, meadows and gardens alongside a brook. Belonging to the Lordship of Bourton, it was at one time in the ownership of the Dean and Chapter of Newark. The hamlet is still a peaceful, contained place.

For many years Draycote had a Baptist chapel. Dated 1811, it was rebuilt in 1869, closed in the late 1930s and is now privately owned. The preachers came on horseback or walked, from Coventry or Rugby. The site was reputed to have been previously occupied by a dance hall!

Draycote has given its name to a surprisingly large number of things: a former pottery; a cattery; transport; Draycote Water, the reservoir of whose 240 hectares 80 are in the parish; and the beautiful nature reserve, Draycote Meadows. Here are the flowers which Shakespeare would have known, 'Daisies Pied, Ladysmocks and Cuckoo Buds'.

🍁 BRAILES

The village of Brailes lies tucked snugly into the southernmost tip of Warwickshire, and is divided into two, Upper and Lower, straggling both sides of the curving main road running between Shipston-on-Stour and Banbury.

Brailes Hill, the second highest point in Warwickshire, rises soft and green towards the fringes of the Gloucestershire wolds, and is surmounted by a distinctive group of trees. The real name of this is Highwall Coppice, but to all Brailes locals it is simply Brailes Clump.

On the other side of the village street is the man-made mound of Castle Hill, a dome topped earthwork, once an ancient burial ground. At one time this was used as a base for a castle of the motte and bailey type, but no trace of it now remains. The walk across the fields and the climb to be 'King of the Castle' is a popular weekend pastime for Brailes' youngsters and their parents.

In medieval times Brailes was a thriving and bustling market town, the third largest in the county, and its former prosperity is reflected in the fine church of St George in Lower Brailes, referred to as the Cathedral of the Feldon. It has many points of interest and there are stones from the 11th century built into its 14th century walls. However, like many such churches it suffered somewhat at the hands of the Victorians.

Feldon is the name given to this rich area of fertile farming land, and aerial surveys have revealed traces of earlier roads and villages where now there are productive fields. Walk to the top of the hill, and look at the panorama below, and remains of the old ridge and furrow cultivation are very evident all around.

In addition to the fine parish church, the village is fortunate in its Catholic church of St Peter and St Paul, built in 1726 in the upper part of a barn adjoining a farm. It is so well hidden, in fact, that the casual visitor would have difficulty in finding it.

There is also a Methodist chapel, built in what was referred to as the 'Italianate' style in 1863.

A few notables have lived here, and not too many of the infamous. Perhaps the most famous son was William de Brailes, who was one of only two known English artists responsible for some of the beautiful and delicate work on illuminated 13th century manuscripts. His work has been exhibited at many specialist museums and art galleries, but can be seen on permanent view at the Fitzwilliam Museum, Cambridge. It is signed with his own 'portrait', a tiny, bent figure with a shaven head.

Another notable was the doctor who served this village for

more than 34 years. Dr Findlay first came to Brailes in 1894. What was truly remarkable about Dr Findlay was that he was a keen amateur photographer in those early days when you had to get beneath a black cloth and photograph on to a black glass plate. Dr Findlay was always asking people he met on the road to 'hold still'. When he died in 1928, he left behind a most precious legacy in the form of a photographic record of Brailes.

The most infamous resident was undoubtedly Nance Austin, the Brailes witch, who lived alone, and had a familiar in the form of a cat. Her speciality was levitation. Recent restoration in Nance's old cottage wall brought forth the remains of an old chimney sacrifice and one of her ancient shoes!

🍁 BRINKLOW

The village green and St John the Baptist church, Brinklow.

Brinklow is a village which goes back to pre Roman times as shown by the prominent mound which can be seen riding above the church. The 'Tump' as it is known locally has, on a clear day,

33

magnificent views of the surrounding towns and countryside and is well worth the climb involved to get to the top. The village today is noted for its location on the Roman Fosse Way and is a natural stopping place for tourists.

The oldest building in Brinklow is the church of St John the Baptist. Monks from Kenilworth Abbey built it and the first rector was appointed in 1252. As the church stands on the lower slopes of the 'Tump' it rises the height of two men towards the altar. The tower and Lady Chapel were added after the terrible 'Black Death' hit the village. In early times there were no seats in the church. The present furniture is Victorian. Around the church, coloured shields tell the story of those people and institutions associated with its history. On a fine day one would be rewarded by browsing in the churchyard, where an interesting headstone can be found to the memory of a deaf and dumb woodcutter, showing a bundle of faggots, a woodsman's glove, an axe and a gorse hook. Beneath is inscribed:

> This man his character to sum,
> From infancy was deaf and dumb,
> His understanding yet was clear,
> His heart was upright and sincere,
> He chiefly got his livelihood
> By faggoting and selling wood,
> Till death The Conqueror of all,
> Gave the feller himself a fall.

Over the centuries the great houses of Coombe Abbey, Newbold Revel and Town Thorns, when in full glory and entertaining many guests, employed many villagers. Basket weaving, candlemaking and the manufacture of silk took place in the village itself and the development of the canal and railway added to the prosperity of the village.

Modern Brinklow has lost its railway station and the canal now brings pleasure craft rather than working barges. Some 1,500 people make their home here and the village has a good variety of houses both ancient and modern, this meeting of old and new giving the village both charm and vitality. Around the old village green cottages have been 'gentrified' and the village centre benefits from being within a conservation area. The colourful village sign was made locally and erected in 1999; it depicts Brinklow life through the ages.

As in all villages the school has always been at the centre of village life. Unfortunately Brinklow's school was closed in 1996 and the old school building is now used as an annexe to the primary school in Monks Kirby.

Brinklow is well known for its hospitality having within its centre no fewer than four public houses: The White Lion, The Raven, The Dun Cow and The Bull's Head, all interesting buildings and containing their own slice of village history. Along the wide main shopping street many changes have taken place in recent years. Food shops and garages that over the years served the village well have closed, a pottery and specialist antiques shops have replaced them.

❧ BROOM

Broom is a small village in the Parish of Bidford-on-Avon, not far from the Vale of Evesham. Having a population of just over 400 and 152 houses, it is a compact little village.

The buildings are a mixture of ancient and modern, some of them being 16th century. The earliest of these is said to be The Broom Tavern, which was built as a farmhouse. With its timber framing and red brick in-fill, this building when floodlit, makes an impressive sight. Another old building is The Broom Hall Inn, also built as a farmhouse and dated 1577.

Earlier than either of these was the Mill, said to have been started by the Monks of Worcester. There used to be two mills under one roof, and these were mentioned in the Domesday Book in 1086. There are now approximately 40 houses on the site.

The Mill stood on the banks of the river Arrow, which flows gently past the western side of the village. The Arrow rises near Birmingham in the Licky Hills and after flowing down past

The 16th century Broom Hall Inn

Broom, joins the Avon about two miles downstream.

Before the bridge was built over the river in about 1900, the river had to be crossed by a ford near the Mill. One horse and cart got swept away in the current, when the water ran high. That first river bridge was finished just as a bad flood came, and it was washed away. Its replacement lasted until 1964, when a stronger bridge and wider road was needed to take so much traffic.

The railway came to Broom in 1866, when the Evesham to Redditch line was completed. This was a boon not only to Broom, but to the surrounding villages too, and was a great loss when it closed in 1962. Now, Broom Junction is a Council yard, and the old railway cuttings have become like nature reserves.

In Mill Lane stood the small church of St Matthew, now a private dwelling. This was built in 1868.

Broom is one of the villages mentioned in the verse by William Shakespeare (see Temple Grafton). This is 'Beggarly Broom', though anyone walking round the village will find this hard to believe today.

🍁 BULKINGTON

The village of Bulkington lies to the north of Coventry in the Borough of Nuneaton and Bedworth. In the Domesday Book, Bulkington is called Bockintone and it seems likely that Anglo-Saxon settlers were attracted by the higher, well-drained land and the plentiful supply of water from the many springs, which abound to this day.

Farming is still an important economic activity in the countryside which surrounds Bulkington. By the time of the Enclosure Acts ribbon weaving had become the major occupation of the villagers. George Eliot knew Bulkington well and referred to it as Raveloe in her book of the cottage weaver, *Silas Marner*.

In 1801 the population was over 1,300, but the fact that there was no coal under Bulkington restricted industrial development and the village remained in a rural setting. Today there are over 9,000 inhabitants with the majority of the workers commuting to the surrounding towns and cities.

Christian worship was likely in Bulkington before the Norman Conquest. The parish church of St James dates from the 13th century, though documents prove that a church existed on the site in 1143. A fragment of this earlier church is incorporated in the modern porch. The 15th century tower houses a fine peal of bells, four of them being over 300 years old. The remaining four are modern. These are rung by an active team of bell-ringers.

In the church are several examples of the work of the amateur sculptor, Richard Hayward, who lived at the manor house Weston Hall in the 18th century. A particularly fine piece is the font sculpted in Cararra marble, which stands upon a plinth bearing this inscription: 'This fragment of ancient Numidian marble was imported by Richard Hayward and given to this church MDCCLXXXIX'.

In 1821 box pews were placed in the body of the church, and they bore the scars inflicted upon them by generations of Bulkington children bored by long sermons. The old pews were removed some years ago and replaced by more modern pews from a redundant church.

The churchyard is noted for its table tombs, and one which stands to the right of the porch is to the memory of Mr and Mrs Johnson, uncle and aunt of George Eliot whom she portrayed as Uncle and Aunt Pullet in her book *The Mill on the Floss*. Devotees of George Eliot travel to Bulkington from all over the world just to look at this tomb.

The manor house, Weston Hall, was built in the reign of Elizabeth I, by the De La Zouche family. Today the Hall is a hotel but retains the original Elizabethan facade. The stable-block, added in the late 19th century by Francis Newdegate, lord of the manor was restored in 1988 from a ruinous state to provide high-class dwellings.

The old infants' school in the centre of the village closed and thanks to the energy of a committee of volunteers it is now the 'Village Centre', used for social activities, meetings and educational courses. Also on the site is a police office, the clinic, a pre-school and a nursery, while the local doctor's practice has built a new surgery in the school grounds.

❧ Burton Dassett

The parish of Burton Dassett is located in the south of the county close to the borders of Oxfordshire and Northamptonshire. It is made up of the villages of Northend, Knightcote, Temple Herdewyke and the smaller communities of Burton Dassett and Little Dassett.

Burton Dassett is the oldest part of the parish with its part Norman church, to be found just outside the area of the Dassett Hills, which is now a country park run by Warwickshire County Council. In years gone by this was a wild natural area with a post windmill at its summit, and also a stone beacon which is still there and visible for many miles around. 'Ghosts' seen on the hills have been put down to vapour rising from the natural springs there. In living memory stone was quarried there. A bridlepath, Mill Lane, leads up to the hills from Northend village.

Northend village is at the foot of the Dassett Hills and has a variety of old stone houses and also many modern properties. The first council houses were built in the 1930s. During the Second World War many evacuees came from Coventry and London and Land Army girls from Birmingham. A small unit in the village made tools for munitions factories and the barrage balloon over Coventry was clearly visible from the Dassett Hills. Although the heavy bombing was very near at Coventry, the closest disaster was the crash of a 'Flying Fortress' bomber.

Midway between Northend and Knightcote is Granslet Pool with a paved base, where horses and carts were driven through for the wooden wheels of the carts to have a 'soak' and so not lose their iron rims.

Knightcote village has, over the years, lost its Royal Oak public house and school (both now residences). One row of thatched houses remains, however, the only thatched properties in the parish. Knightcote has a new village hall, a Methodist chapel, and the farming includes a dairy herd as well as arable, sheep and cattle.

Just outside the village is Stockwell Spring – similar saline water to Leamington Spa water. Two brick and stone slab standpipe covers remain in the village – a reminder of the water supply from the Dassett Hills. This water still feeds cattle troughs on the Knightcote side of the hills and at least one resident collects water from here for a 'decent cup of tea'!

Temple Herdewyke is a new village (Army married quarters). The Army Camp site was agricultural land prior to the Second World War, and many older parishioners were employed on the farms and in the farmhouses there.

Within the parish boundaries there is an Anglo-Saxon settlement and burial ground. At Little Dassett there was a Roman Catholic chapel – known now as Chapel Barn. The Battle of Edgehill was fought on the boundary of the parish in 1642 and the whole area is steeped in history.

Not much is known of John Kimbell who, over 500 years ago, left land for the benefit of the inhabitants of Northend and Knightcote. Locally it is understood he was down on his luck and was given food in Northend and shelter in Knightcote. This was obviously not forgotten and the children and senior citizens still benefit – albeit with cash instead of coal at Christmas, but every household still receives a loaf of bread at New Year.

❦ CHERINGTON & STOURTON

Cherington House is an 18th century building which used to belong to the Dickins family, who had the picturesque habit of planting a chestnut tree to celebrate the birth of each new member of the family. As one Mrs Dickins had 13 children, they made an impressive row. Sadly they were chopped down in the Second World War. A more recent Mrs Dickins was a great supporter of music in the church and is still remembered by villagers as an exacting choir-mistress. How long has the family lived here? In the north aisle stands a handsome, carved 13th century tomb, whose effigy has not been identified.

Weston Park was once a fine Elizabethan house which must have been neglected, as heirs of the estate died out. It was demolished in 1834 to make way for an impressive Victorian pile. Alas, this lasted only a hundred years; its stone was used to build the former Banbury Police Station, while the furniture and pictures went to the United States.

Thatched cottages look so attractive yet they are not always comfortable to live in. Daddy Berrows was a real village character who kept a shop in a thatched cottage, only one wall of which now remains. He had a lot of trouble with his thatch. First he spread tarpaulin over the top. When that proved inadequate, he stretched more tarpaulin underneath the thatch. Perhaps it is not surprising that he was never seen without his hat on, even indoors. Although he always had a huge roaring fire in the hearth in the winter, the villagers said that the house never went up in flames because the thatch was much too wet to catch fire!

🍁 CHESTERTON

Chesterton is a very small hamlet, with a mostly 14th century church but no shop or pub. It is cut by the Fosse Way, and there are still signs of the Roman settlement. It used to have a large manor house on the hill behind the church, occupied by the Peyto family for centuries until 1802, when it was pulled down.

It was Sir Edward Peyto who built the windmill in 1632 and the watermill about the same time. The windmill is fully restored, and open to the public every two years. The watermill has still kept all the millworkings, and is also being restored. The pond itself has been dredged out and is now used for trout fishing.

🍁 CHURCH LAWFORD & KINGS NEWNHAM

The villages of Church Lawford and Kings Newnham are linked by an old sandstone bridge spanning the river Avon which separates them. Both villages have histories going back to the Roman occupation and before.

Church Lawford, recorded as Leileford in the Domesday Book lies off the A428 Rugby–Coventry road. The church, dedicated to St Peter, stands on high ground overlooking the Avon and was rebuilt in 1873/4 on the site where the 14th century church once stood.

Close to the church is Manor Farm with its beautiful timber framed Tudor house, one of the oldest buildings in the village. The Old Rectory and The Old Smithy are also interesting, especially the inn with its low beamed ceilings and panelled walls which are enhanced with brass hangings and ornaments, giving a warm and friendly welcome to visitors. Across the road from the inn is the Reading Room which was bequeathed to the village by the Townsend sisters over 100 years ago and is now administered by a Board of Trustees. The Room is well used by village organisations.

There are people in the village today who remember when

there was a blacksmith's shop in Smithy Lane, with the smell of horses and hot metal and a smith who chased away the saucy children who sneaked into his shop to pump the bellows, by cracking a horse whip behind them.

After crossing the bridge to Kings Newnham, or Newnham Regis, as it used to be called, there are three ponds on the right-hand side of the lane. These ponds, or stews, were made for the monks of Kenilworth Abbey 1,000 years ago, where they kept stocks of fish to supplement their larders. Today the ponds are the home for a variety of water fowl and each year a pair of swans breeds there.

The Hall on the left of the road is a fine 18th century house, now a farm. In the grounds are two listed buildings, an ancient dovecote and the tower of St Laurence's church. The church was probably built by the Kenilworth monks, but the nave and chancel were destroyed in 1794. The bells were taken to St Mary's church, Monks Kirby, and the font taken to adorn the garden of The Hall.

Around 1850 Lord John Scott inherited the estate and one day after heavy rain, it was observed that water in the rick-yard, which had formerly been the churchyard, drained away remarkably quickly. After investigations near the old tower, a water-filled underground vault was discovered containing several lead lined coffins. One coffin contained the body of Lady Audry Leigh who died in 1640 and could not have been more than 17 years old. Plates on other coffins showed that they contained the bodies of Francis, Earl of Chichester, Lady Chichester, Lord Dunsmore and Sir John Anderson. However, the most interesting and intriguing coffin was unnamed and had in it the remains of a man who had been beheaded, the head being separately prepared for burial and laid with the body. Around the neck was a black silk ribbon embroidered with the initials T.B. This and the other bodies had been embalmed and covered with rosemary and other herbs, but once the coffins had been opened and the remains exposed to the air, they rapidly disintegrated.

Lord John Scott ordered the the coffins be resealed and replaced with a zinc cover over the vault and a brass tomb plate.

The plate was later removed to protect it from vandalism and is now kept in The Hall.

At nearby Little Lawford (Lilleford in Domesday Book) used to stand Little Lawford Hall. Here in 1780 Sir Theodosius Boughton was murdered by his brother-in-law, Captain Donellan, who mixed poison with his medicine, hoping to inherit the estate, but instead was hanged at Warwick. Thus the male line of the Boughton's was ended.

Most of Little Lawford Hall was demolished about 1790 and the present building is early 19th century. This is thought to have been the stable block of the old hall which was reputed to be haunted by the ghost of One-Handed Boughton, a forebear who lost an arm in the reign of Queen Elizabeth I, and drives a ghostly coach and six across the grounds.

🍁 CHURCHOVER

Churchover is situated near the Warwickshire/Leicestershire border, north of Rugby. It is set on a hill, overlooking the Swift valley, in pleasant pastoral land.

The church, dedicated to the Holy Trinity, was mostly restored in the late 19th century. It has a 15th century tower, a Norman font with a cover dated 1673 and two monuments from the 16th century. One of these commemorates the Dixwell family, who lived at Coton House, which is a mile from the village. John Dixwell (1607–1689) was one of the signatories to the death warrant of Charles I. At the restoration of the monarchy, he was forced to flee the country and became one of the founding fathers of Newhaven, Connecticut, New England.

A Manor House has stood on the Coton House site since Saxon times, but after the Norman Conquest it passed into the king's hands. In 1291 it was held in part by the monks of Coombe Abbey, who built a monastic grange. King Henry VIII granted the manor to the Duchess of Richmond and it passed, through various hands, to the Dixwells. In 1787 Abraham Grimes had a new house erected after a design by Samuel Wyatt. Francis

Arkwright was the last lord of the manor and at the turn of the century Mr Arthur James became a tenant. Mrs Arthur James was godmother to Queen Elizabeth The Queen Mother, and the oak screen at the entrance to the chancel in Churchover church was erected to the memory of Mrs James by Her Majesty.

In 1949, after the death of Mrs James, Coton House became an Apprentice Residence for the British Thomson-Houston Company (later AEI) and then in 1970 it was bought by the Post Office as a Management Training College.

Many years ago, the occupation of most of the inhabitants was agricultural, on the farms or as estate workers at Coton House. Later, when the engineering works came to Rugby, a large number went to work in the factories. The farms have now dwindled to two.

The village school was closed in 1973 and the children now travel to Monks Kirby and Rugby for their education. The building is now used as a Community Centre. The village shop, which had stood in the same place for probably about 100 years, has closed, together with the post office.

About ¼ mile outside the village, by the lane leading to the next parish of Harborough Magna, a North Sea Gas distribution installation was built in the early 1970s. Landscaping has helped to obscure the extensive pipework and valves, but it is still something of a blot on this very rural scene.

🍁 CLAVERDON

Claverdon, with a population of 1,245 in 1986, sits astride the B4095 Warwick to Redditch road, in the old Barlichway Hundred and Arden Forest. Mentioned in the Domesday Book as Clavendone, the Early English 'Claefer Dun' or Clover Hill, pronounced in living memory as 'Clardon', still has plenty of clover to be seen.

Claverdon can boast two features which are poles apart in their uniqueness. One is the much photographed forge, said to date from the 17th century, with a horseshoe shaped archway for

The 17th century forge at Claverdon

which Mr Darwin Galton was responsible. The other, to be found in the Church Centre, is an embroidered panel approximately 9 by 5 feet, designed by an embroideress and executed by herself and eight friends who were all keen amateurs when they started. It depicts village life in 1980.

A very distant ancestor of the late Princess of Wales (who was Lady Diana Spencer) has a magnificent monument in the church, which he had built for himself. He was Thomas Spencer, second son of Sir John Spencer of Althorp, born about 1547 and died at age 82 in 1629. It had been a wise move on his part to have a monument erected, as with no immediate family his kinsfolk did not bother to add the date of death to it. This same Thomas Spencer was probably responsible for building the Stone Manor, an unusual three storey structure about which there is much conjecture. Pevsner asserts that it is a defensive tower-house, rare in the Midlands.

While Thomas boasts a fine monument, his funeral cannot compare with that of the scientist and explorer, Sir Francis Galton, who, it was said, 'was the most illustrious person to be buried in the Church yard', in 1911. He was a cousin of Charles Darwin, father of eugenics, developed identification by finger-prints and an early work, *Meteorographica* (1863) contains the basis of modern weather charts.

Schooling, first mentioned in the Rate Book for 1733, continues today in the village, in a modern building opened in 1966 to replace the National School of 1847. Mr Enoch H. Belcher was appointed Headmaster in March 1876, straight from college. He stayed until he retired 43 years later and lived on in the village until his death. He was a true 'character'. He organised most of the clubs and activities in the village, formed a brass band, leading and conducting it and started the cricket club which still flourishes today. When the Parish Council held its first meeting in December 1894, he was elected as the first Chairman. For many years he was church organist, too!

The church, with dedication to St Michael and All Angels and sister parish at Preston Bagot, may not be outstanding architecturally and was much restored by the Victorians, but has a most calming and restorative atmosphere for all who cross its threshold.

Geologically interesting is Tattle Bank, an area of sandy gravel forming a capping to the underlying red clay of Keuper marl. The gravel was formed during the Ice Age some 250,000 years ago, when two great glaciers invaded this area, from north-west and north-east.

🍁 CLIFTON-UPON-DUNSMORE

The village of Clifton-upon-Dunsmore is situated some 2½ miles east of Rugby on the western slopes of a fairly steep hill which, at its highest point, is just over 400 feet. Near to the village is Dow Bridge at which the three counties of Warwickshire, Northamptonshire and Leicestershire meet. One and a half miles north of Clifton are the extensive remains of a great Roman military station called Tripontium.

The village is said to take its name from its location – 'Cliffe' in Saxon signifying rocky ground, and 'Dunsmore' on the top of a hill.

During the reign of Edward the Confessor (1042–1066) Clifton was in the possession of the Sheriff of Warwick, Alwinus Viceomes or Alwyn, founder of the Arden family. Alwyn gave his land at Clifton 'for the health of his soul' to the priory of St Michael's of Coventry, which had been founded by the Earl of Mercia, Earl Leofric husband of Lady Godiva. It is very likely that the monks of Coventry built a dwelling and chapel on the present site of the church.

As the population of Clifton village increased in the 14th century, so the church grew in size, the nave, south and north aisles being added in that century. It is probable that towards the close of the 14th century the church was rededicated to the glory of the Blessed Virgin Mary. It is now commonly called St Mary's.

The large squat tower was the last main part of the church to be built in the 16th century of sandstone. Originally it possessed a tall, tapering spire which is thought to have collapsed in a great storm and demolished several dwellings in what is now Church Street.

The tower has a west window above which used to be clearly visible a curious muzzled bear figure – the outline of it can still be seen. It is likely that the sculpture is the crest of an old influential village family called the Barfords, their crest being a bear sable.

There is an ancient couplet relating to the bear inscribed on the court roll of the Manor, giving a warning against the dissipated habits of the time:

> 'Ye yonge men of Cliftone
> Of Ye Lyon Bewayre
> If your wish to be happy
> Turn in at Ye Bayre.'

The Lion Inn was one of two public houses in Clifton, the village hall now standing on its site. The couplet was advising men to turn into church rather than frequent The Lion. The other Clifton public house, The Bull Inn, once a Hanoverian farmhouse, is still thriving in Main Street. Legend tells of an underground passage leading from The Bull to the church – for what purpose one can only guess!

The population of Clifton rose swiftly in the 19th century. In 1841 it was 364 and 585 in 1881. There is evidence from the census records of a good deal of overcrowding and actual housing shortage during this period. The coming of the railway to Rugby in 1838 and the opening of the Clifton Mill experimental crossing in 1864 had a profound effect upon the village.

🍁 COLESHILL

Coleshill dates back to Saxon times, but it gained in importance when it became a staging-post in coaching days along the main London to Holyhead route. At that time it boasted more than 20 inns.

The most notable feature is the handsome church, built on the site of one which existed in the time of Edward the Confessor. The font is a rare example of Norman sculpture. Set in the floor of the chancel is a brass figure of the first vicar of the Reformation, John Fenton. This is a 'must' for brass rubbers, because his right hand displays five fingers and a thumb.

Outside on Church Hill stand the stocks, unique in Warwickshire because they combine a whipping-post and a pillory. In the 18th century they were prominent in front of an arched Market Hall in the middle of the road. The Market Hall was demolished in 1865 and moved to a building further down the hill, known as the 'Institute'. During the last few years this old building has been lovingly restored as part museum, part meeting place, and renamed The Old Market Hall, and the pillory repositioned outside.

Famous local people include Simon Digby, awarded the manor of Coleshill in 1496 by Henry VII after the battle of Bosworth, and his wife Alice, who established the first charity in the parish for poor children.

A more infamous character was one John Wynn, owner of a cinema on the site of the present Cameo Suite. He operated a transmitter in the roof of the building during the Second World War and was caught giving information to the Germans.

Stories abound of two ghosts, one of a lady who appears on the stairs in Queen Anne House in the High Street and one of a highwayman who is reputed to have hidden in the cellar of a cottage where now stands an estate agent's office, also in the High Street. He does not appear, but can be heard moving about in the building.

Strangest of all perhaps is the elephant that choked on a mangold and expired outside The Bell Inn on the Birmingham Road, and is buried under what is now the Sons of Rest bowling green.

🍁 CORLEY

At the start of the 20th century a rector and his family, by the name of Hamilton, lived at Corley Rectory. In 1942, 40 years on, the Rector's son had a dream in which he relived his childhood days. So deep were his thoughts he felt compelled to put them into verse, and called it *Corley 1902*. This is what he wrote:

> For this is Corley Lane, I know by heart
> That bend, that slope, driving the governess cart,
> And Gipsy, stubborn pony, knows them too;
> In each unchanging house I know who's who;
> Here at her gate good kindly Mrs Wall
> With the twisted smile will answer if I call;
> Here wizened Pettifor lives, and Steeley there,
> Silent, important man, the carrier,
> Who from his high-wheeled cart looks grimly down
> On the slow-motion road, full five miles long, to town.

What a gem of rural England can be envisaged, and what a wealth of information is revealed. The motor car had not arrived, the horse held sway, and the knowing of who's who was a true picture of Corley in 1902.

Hall Farm, which George Eliot so wonderfully describes in her book *Adam Bede* was struck by disaster in the 1920s. The dreaded disease Foot and Mouth was confirmed, thus destroying a lifetime's work. Happily, and to the relief of people with stock, it was self-contained, and was the only attack in Warwickshire.

The rich sanded Corley Rocks, with its wealth of bracken and bramble, was a wonderful playground for children, who came in droves from nearby Coventry and Bedworth. The woods, too, were a big attraction, especially at bluebell time.

In 1996 the Church school closed and the children from Corley now attend school in the neighbouring village of Fillongley, where the school has been renamed Bournebrook School.

The old school has been sold and converted into a private residence. Several farms which were once viable units have been sold. In many cases the land has been added to neighbouring farms and the houses and farm buildings sold for private occupation. New businesses have been opened in the village, including two garden centres, a cattery, a dog training centre, stables and a livery yard, all indicative of the present affluent lifestyle in which we live.

It was after the First World War that the carrier's slow-motion road became the route to the booming town of Coventry and began to draw people away. The volume of traffic on today's M6 motorway has increased dramatically during the past decade. More villagers travel daily to their places of employment in neighbouring cities and beyond, thus increasing the number of motor vehicles on local roads.

🍁 COUGHTON

The modern village of Coughton straddles the A435, Icknield Street, two miles north of the market town of Alcester. The bulk of the village lies to the west of the main road along Coughton Lane and Wike Lane and to the east along Coughton Fields.

The ancient village, mentioned in the Domesday Book under the name Coctune, lay between the Forest of Arden and Feckenham Forest. In 1300 the whole village west of the river Arrow, a tributary of Shakespeare's Avon, was taken into Feckenham Forest by King John. At the corner of Coughton Fields and the A435, surrounded by railings, are the remains of an ancient stone cross marking the end of Feckenham Forest. Travellers are said to have given thanks here for a safe passage through the Forest.

There are still several examples of ancient cottages, albeit much modernised. Some of the houses in the village are Georgian, some Victorian and the rest modern. Long before the Tudor village there was a Roman settlement called Wike or Wyke, hence Wike Lane.

The Manor House, Coughton Court, belonged to the Throckmorton family who gave it to the nation in 1945, but who retained the contents and a portion of the house as their residence. The present house dates from the beginning of the 16th century and was built either on the site of, or as an enlargement to an existing house. It is now a National Trust property and open to the public.

The parish church, next door to the Court, was built by Sir Robert Throckmorton between 1486 and 1518. It has a peal of 6 bells which were restored in 1976 and are still carried in their original wooden frame. The Roman Catholic church and presbytery lie at the southern end of the Court driveway and were built towards the end of the 19th century.

The thriving village school which serves the surrounding area, was originally housed in an ancient barn, now a residential home for the elderly, along the main road towards Studley. It was eventually moved to a purpose-built Victorian school house in Wike Lane. When this school became too small, the 'new' school, dating from the mid 1950s, was built in Coughton Lane. Further up Wike Lane lies the old railway station built in 1868 and now enlarged as a private house called 'Booking Hall'.

The village still has two churches, a bus service and a pub (although technically this is in the parish of Sambourne). Missing from the last century are the railway, the shop and the post office.

🍁 CUBBINGTON

Cubbington was mentioned in the Domesday Book of 1086, the first spelling being Cubitone. The ancient spelling was Cobynton which was derived from 'town of the descendants of Coba'.

Prior to 1950 the village consisted mainly of small back-to-back cottages with gas lighting and in some cases paraffin lamps. Water was obtained from a pump or well, but in the main street of the village water was drawn from a spring. Communal wash-houses were used, these being allocated to the housewives on a certain day each week. Sewerage was not connected until after the Second World War.

Mr L. B. Thwaites formed his company on its present site in 1938, employing a few men. As Thwaites Limited, there are now over 200 employees, producing dumpers and small excavators which are exported all over the world. Two other local employers are the saw mills which have been in the village for about 100 years, and Stereomatic Limited who manufacture high precision components.

The two churches, Anglican and Methodist, have always played an important part in the village. At one time there was a lot of conflict between them but for several years now they have held united services. From 1792 to 1820, the vicar of St Mary's parish church was the Rev James Austen, the brother of Jane Austen, the famous novelist. During the period 1918–1952, the Rev P. T. Broadway was the vicar and he and his wife did a great deal for the church and the village. One of the roads in the village is named after him. On the north side of the chancel hangs the Abraham Murcott memorial. On the shield is painted 'Abra. Murcott Mariner 1702'. He is reported to have been lost at sea during a dreadful storm.

It is said that two local men going to a football match were involved in an argument and in the fight which followed, one had his earlobe bitten off. From then on, men of the village were nicknamed 'Cubbington Earbiters'.

There was great excitement in the village on a morning in early November 1605, as the sound of galloping horses had been heard in the middle of the night. The next morning the news broke that on 5th November 1605 after Guy Fawkes was discovered and seized at the Houses of Parliament, Robert Catesby and some of his conspirators had set off to meet their confederates at Dunchurch. From there Catesby and his followers made a wild dash by night for Wales, riding through Princethorpe, Weston-under-Wetherley and Cubbington to Warwick, where they stole horses from the castle.

During the Second World War the villagers opened their already over-crowded homes to evacuees from Coventry, Birmingham and London. Some of these evacuees have remained and made their homes in the village. Mr Horace Lloyd and his firemen crew were awarded the British Empire Medal for their work on the night of the Coventry Blitz, 14th November 1940.

🍁 CURDWORTH

The name Curdworth evolved from Credeword, 'Creda's Settlement'. The original settlement was a Saxon clearing in the Forest of Arden near the river Tame.

The parish church of St Nicholas dates from 1165 though there was probably a Saxon church on the same site before then. In 1895 Lord Norton restored the church at his own expense and Prime Minister Gladstone visited to view progress of the work. There are many interesting features: medieval wall paintings, a 13th century ten feet long dug-out chest, carved from a single tree trunk, and a 15th century silver bell, given by a traveller lost in the forest who was guided home by a bell tinkling in the church. In the floor of the nave is a memorial to Cornelius and Anne Ford, of nearby Dunton Hall. Their daughter Sarah was the 'dear honoured mother' of Dr Johnson.

The church is on rising ground, dominating the village, and is adjacent to a rectangular site which is possibly the site of a very early manor house. Below this is 'The Battlefield', a tree-lined hollow reputedly the scene of the first skirmish of the Civil War in 1642. Sir William Dugdale guided soldiers through the forest towards the king at Nottingham, taking arms and supplies. Parliamentarians pursued them and crossed the bridge over the Tame and a battle ensued near the church. The king's men supposedly won.

Curdworth has evolved from being a rural area, with agriculture and later the Severn Trent Drainage Board dominating the economy, to its present somewhat undefined status. There is now much less dependency on farming although quite a lot of flat, open land around the village is intensively farmed, producing wheat, barley and latterly, rape. With growing development the village has become a 'dormitory' for nearby Birmingham, especially since the advent of the M42 and access to the M5, but there is still a friendly village atmosphere and feeling of continuity with the past.

There are many charming old cottages. Three cottages at the corner of Farthing Lane were originally a timber-framed Tudor farmhouse and later a coaching-inn called The Royal Oak – the oakleaf motif is still above the large inglenook fireplace in the middle cottage. Although modernised, some interesting internal features have been retained. Two are owned by the Water Authority and the smallest is privately owned. Curdworth Hall Farm, about 300 years old, is built on a base of medieval sandstone. Some of its windows are of hand-blown glass and some iron-framed, with butterfly catches. There are large stables and this could have been a 'Bush House', or inn, for travellers using the old turnpike road. The small pond is believed to have been the fish pool for the original Curdworth Hall and the moat is clearly defined – probably a status symbol, rather than for defence! Another two cottages about 250 years old were occupied by the blacksmith and family and until 1975 there was an adjoining forge, now replaced by a modern house. It is thought that the Civil War skirmish was partly fought on the rear garden of these cottages.

🍁 DOSTHILL & WHATELEY

Before the Second World War, Dosthill was quite a small village consisting of a cluster of farms, old cottages, the vicarage and Norman chapel, grouped quite picturesquely around the church at the top of the hill, connected by the High Street to some rather depressing coal miners' houses at the lower end of the village. The High Street itself was a rather grand name for a straggle of diverse houses, including some old cottages, some short terraces, and a few detached houses built mainly during the 1930s.

The chief employment was either mining (the mines being situated away from the village), or clayworking, there being a proliferation of brickworks in the area due to the rich supply of clay which was readily available. In contrast, there is also a unique outcrop of volcanic rock, and this was quarried for many years, leaving behind a hole filled with water nearly 100 feet deep, which is now used for sub-aqua diving. Many of the older people still living in the village remember the aerial buckets transporting the stone from the quarry, across the main road to the stonecrusher which was sited at the brickworks.

A cruck barn at Church Farm, Dosthill

55

The countryside to the west of the village is known as the Roundhills, a series of slopes levelling out into the valley of the river Tame. Being mainly unfit for cultivation it is ideal for rambles, and after winter snow, for tobogganing. The view from the highest point is magnificent, and the water meadows in the valley are extensive.

Since the Second World War a tremendous change has taken place, slowly at first with the building of a housing estate on farmland, but accelerating since the 1960s. Despite all these changes, Dosthill has somehow retained its village atmosphere.

All but two of the brickworks have disappeared, those remaining being tucked away and having no visual impact on the village. The old beehive kilns which had been allowed to crumble away, and the derelict land surrounding them, have been replaced by modern but attractive private housing estates, and the miners' houses have given way to comfortable accommodation for the elderly.

The oldest surviving building in the village is the Norman chapel, originally a chapel of ease, and used variously for church services before the present church was completed in 1872, and as a Dame School before the present school was built in 1887.

Other buildings of interest include a cruck barn belonging to Church Farm, and used until recently as a dancing school. Dosthill Hall, a Georgian house which was once a health spa, was allowed to fall into disrepair, but has been rescued and beautifully restored by its present owners. Mountside, a large late Georgian or early Victorian house, was built by the main landowner and one-time squire of the village, Mr Cheatle. The last survivor of this well-known family in the village was a maiden lady, Miss Maud Cheatle, who died in the 1960s. She was instrumental in the setting up of the local youth club, giving them land and money which has resulted in the club becoming probably the wealthiest in the country.

Whateley is just a hamlet atop an even higher hill than Dosthill, and just under two miles distant. Its old name was Wheatley, and for some years it was known by both names. In direct contrast to the larger village, it has shrunk rather than expanded.

The surrounding countryside has scarcely changed, there is no pub, church, or shop, and Whateley remains a pretty and peaceful, out-of-this-world spot, unspoilt and truly rural.

DUNCHURCH

Dunchurch, or Don Cerce as it was known in 1086, stands on the old coach road from London and no doubt this is the reason for the 27 alehouses it once boasted! Now there are two, The Dun Cow, an old coaching inn and The Green Man public house. The inn where the Gunpowder Plot conspirators took refuge on their flight from justice is now a private house named Guy Fawkes House.

The old gaol, which was pulled down in 1972, once held overnight miscreants but the stocks on the village green are the only reminders of those days. The last person to be locked up was Peter Murcott who spent his night in gaol supping beer through a straw from a keg outside the window, probably left by his friends!

The parish church of St Peter, Dunchurch

Standing at the crossroads is a magnificent statue commemorating Lord John Scott, once a local landowner. The statue was surrounded by iron railings which were taken for scrap metal during the Second World War. Each Christmas the statue is appropriately dressed by anonymous persons.

The Almshouses which were built in the 17th century have retained their old world look but have been fully modernised inside. Adjoining them are two private houses originally the boys school and the schoolmaster's house. The school for girls and infants was built in the churchyard in 1837. Some of the children came from very large families and started their education at three years of age. It is an interesting fact that when the school was demolished in 1929, the land reverted back to being the churchyard and so quite a number of people are buried literally where they went to school!

The parish church of St Peter, first mentioned in the Domesday Book of 1086, is still well attended and the many memorials in the church testify to the esteem in which it was held by previous inhabitants.

In 1987 the village was 'twinned' with a village in France called Ferrieries en Brie. The friendships have grown over the years and there are at least two official group visits made each year between the villages. Much celebration takes place on these occasions.

Dunchurch is a good place to enjoy good food or to stay, for there are hotels, restaurants and cafes clustered around the centre of the village. The visitor in a hurry is also able to enjoy 'fast-food' from any of the three take-aways. A further 16 shops cater for the needs of visitors and residents alike.

The smithy, about which Longfellow wrote his poem, *The Village Blacksmith*, still stands and is frequently photographed by visitors. It is now a private house called 'The Old Forge'. Although there are many picturesque thatched cottages in Dunchurch there are also modern estates catering for young families. Its position close to the motorway network allows for easy commuting over some surprising distances.

🍁 EARLSWOOD

Earlswood in the Forest of Arden has a romantic ring to it. The first known record of the name came in 1484 when King Richard III granted William Catesby 'an hundred oaks to be taken from the said King's old park of Tanworth or Earlswood in Tanworth within this county'. Only one house in Earlswood predates this: The Moat House, previously known as Cowernes, is a timber framed house dating from 1480 surrounded by a considerably older moat. It is thought that Richard Cowerne lived here in 1387 in an even earlier house protected by the same moat. The National Trust owns the house but it is not open to the public.

It was not until the commencement of building the Birmingham to Stratford-upon-Avon canal in 1783 by Josiah Clowes that Earlswood began to grow as a community. In 1813 plans were drawn up to build three reservoirs to feed the canal system. The Canal Company paid Tanworth Churchwardens £969.8.9d. for 51 acres of Earlswood Common and the reservoirs were completed in 1821.

These reservoirs, known locally as lakes, are the main feature of the area. The engine house built at the end of one lake dominates the landscape and still feeds the canal system with water. Commercial use of the canal ceased in 1936 but it is still in use for pleasure craft. In 1987 up-grading work ordered by the Government Inspector of Dams was carried out on the lakes, thus saving them for the future.

Early in the 20th century charabancs would arrive in Earlswood to disgorge their passengers for a 'day out' by the lakes. Cyclists would come in their hundreds. Local residents provided safe keeping for the bicycles for 2d. and many sold refreshments. Boats could be hired and fishermen lined the banks.

Today there is a flourishing sailing club formed in 1959, and fishermen still enjoy their sport.

Other activities very popular in the area are horse riding and golf. There is endless scope for walking and bird watching. Clowes Wood has been a nature reserve since 1974 and is part of a Site of

Special Scientific Interest which includes New Fallings Coppice and the reservoirs. Birmingham Boys Clubs have a permanent camp site in New Fallings Coppice. Sadly some other woods in the area were lost when the M42 motorway was constructed.

The parish church of St Patrick was built in 1840 with money raised from the sale of land for the reservoirs and rebuilt in 1899. It is situated almost a mile from the centre of the village. A school was later built next to the church and most children travel here by bus.

The post office cum village store, a dress shop and hairdresser situated near The Reservoir Hotel form the nucleus of a very scattered village right on the edge of the county.

Most of the countryside is farmed and there is little industry, only a few small engineering units and a farmhouse cheese factory. Fowlers have been making cheese in Earlswood since 1840 and are the oldest family cheesemakers in the country. The exclusive taste of their cheese is said to be due to the calcium rich water from a 1,000 foot deep well. There are still some houses without mains water or mains sewerage.

🍁 EASENHALL

Tucked away in the north-eastern corner of Warwickshire lies the little village of Easenhall. About 40 houses cluster around an old pub and two farmsteads, one of which has a big 'listed' barn with a high archway, which gives access to the farmyard, and a 200 year old cedar tree. Some of the cottages and semi-detached Victorian houses used to accommodate the families of those working for the great house of Newbold Revel. In fact it is thought that the name Easenhall is derived from the fact that the village is near the eastern lodge of this estate.

Nowadays 'the Revel' is the major training college in the country for prison officers. The population of the village is made up of farmers, old established families and commuters who have been attracted by its unspoilt character, and the fact that it is only four miles from Rugby and seven from Coventry, with easy access to motorways, railways and airports.

The village has no post office, church or school but there is a former Congregational chapel which was sold to the residents some 35 years ago. This tiny building, consisting of one room with no facilities, has become the village hall.

A good community spirit is maintained by participation in the County Best Kept Village Competition, which the village has won several times. In addition events such as barbecues, progressive dinners, bonfire parties, Christmas cheese and wine, carol singing and its annual horticultural show and fete go on through the year. There is also an interdenominational service held every fifth Sunday of the month in the hall led by a visiting clergyman.

Sadly the local Church of England primary school in Harborough Magna that did so much to foster the community spirit was closed a few years ago, but the building is now resounding to the sound of even younger children attending the Earlybirds Nursery, which is flourishing there. The infrequent bus service and the telephone kiosk have been threatened from time to time but they have, up to now, survived.

The Golden Lion is a popular meeting place for locals and tourists alike and retains its character of bygone days when it slaked the thirst of villagers with beer, perhaps brewed in the local brewery, now a private house. The main part of the pub dates back to 1640 and still displays some of its wattle and daub wall. The pub entered the new century with a large extension to provide extra accommodation for its growing clientele.

The only home-grown legend is that of the Pailton Miser who lived in squalor in a tumbledown shack up Cord Lane, but was found, on his death in 1891, to be 'wearing' wads of £1 notes in his trousers!

One may catch a glimpse of the Phantom Horseman in the lanes at dead of night. He is the ghost of One-Handed Boughton who died in Old Lawford Hall, which was later burned down. In an attempt to exorcise his ghost his remains were put into a phial and thrown into a nearby pond but – you never can tell!

🍁 ETTINGTON

Ettington has grown up at the intersection of the two former turnpike roads – the north-south route from Warwick to Moreton-in-Marsh, and the east-west road between Stratford and Banbury. It was originally known as Upper Eatington, when Lower Eatington (once Etyndon, and 1½ miles away) was the main settlement. Here stood the fine old parish church, together with the mill on the river Stour, close by the manor house of the Shirley family. This village disappeared completely at the end of the 18th century when the Shirleys landscaped their estate, and by private Act of Parliament changed the old church into a family chapel.

They gave land for a new church dedicated to Thomas à Becket to be built on the hill at Upper Ettington which was now becoming the larger and more important centre. This church, opened in 1803, was built of poor local stone and only lasted for 100 years. The tower survives, as an interesting landmark, but the rest had to be dismantled and the present parish church, dedicated like the old one to the Holy Trinity, was built at the crossroads in 1903. It is now much quieter and safer here, since the building of the A429 bypass with a roundabout at the western edge of the village. The ruins of the old church in Ettington Park are well worth a visit for their historic interest and beauty.

The village also has a beautiful old Friends' Meeting House built in 1681, which is one of the oldest in the country to have been in continuous use. Ettington was a stronghold of Quakerism in the 17th and 18th centuries, and supporters of the Society of Friends suffered much persecution and hardship. There were also two non-conformist chapels – now converted into houses, and a Wesleyan chapel which has recently been demolished.

A few of the older cottages survive, especially around the Square which was once the hub of the village, but is now a quiet backwater hemmed in by newer houses, many built since the Second World War, as the population has increased. More new housing projects are in hand. Very few people are now employed in farming, though the village is surrounded by good arable land.

The village is proud of its long connection with the Shirley family, which is thought to be the only one in England to have retained ownership of its estates through the male line from Saxon times. The name Saswalo is recorded in the Domesday Book and in the archives of Kenilworth Priory. The family house was handsomely rebuilt in the 19th century in the Victorian Gothic style and is now a prestigious luxury hotel. Change of use seems to have been the fate of many of the older buildings – the smithy, the bakery, the chapels, the toll house, the old school and the old school house (part of which was once the village lock-up), and more recently the butcher's and the greengrocer's, have all been converted into dwelling-houses. Even the old Thomas à Becket tower has been tackled.

There are two public houses – The Chequers and The White Horse – but The Saracen's Head on the old Halford road, and The Nelson Coffee House are both now private houses. The Saracen's Head took its name from the spring in Rookery Lane. Legend has it that a knight and his squire returning from the Crusades stopped by the spring to drink, and that their gory trophy – the head of a Saracen they had slain – fell into the spring and there fossilised, hence its inclusion on the Shirley family crest. The spring is said never to stop flowing even in times of drought, and at one time nearby cottagers obtained their water from it.

🍁 EXHALL

From Ardens Grafton the road drops steeply to the north-west across the valley to the village of Exhall with Oversley Castle and Oversley Woods on the opposing hills. The public footpaths around the village and over the hills are popular and frequently used by ramblers. In olden times the path from Exhall to Oversley was the main route taken by villagers having business or shopping in Alcester. Today this footpath links with the Heart of England Way, a long distance walk stretching from Cannock Chase to Chipping Campden.

Exhall is recorded in the Domesday Book and its history

The village of Exhall

probably goes back to Roman times with Roman coins having been found in the village.

In 1939 a local newspaper stated that the entire working population was employed on the land. Today the traditional farm labourer has ceased to exist and over the past years farm cottages have been modernised and extended to make very desirable residences for professional and business people. One farmer has diversified by tastefully restoring farm buildings into self catering cottages.

Village architecture is varied, reflecting the history and development of the village from Elizabethan to modern times. There are some interesting black and white half-timbered buildings and one farmhouse dating back to Tudor times. Most of the houses stand on steep banks on each side of the road and this adds much to the picturesque quality of the village.

The parish church of St Giles, a peaceful little church and well worth a visit, was dedicated around the year 1130 and was restored in 1862. The nave is 12th century and the chancel is 13th century. A Norman doorway in the nave is now blocked and only visible from the outside. There is a brass beside the altar in memory of John Walsingham and his wife Elenor.

The parish boundary takes in part of the village of Ardens Grafton as far as The Golden Cross, the only public house within the parish and a good one and a half miles from Exhall.

The steep wooded hillside known as Grove Hill, which was previously a motorcycle track, is now a nature reserve.

❧ FARNBOROUGH

The village of Farnborough was originally called Fernberge or 'the little hill of ferns'. At the time of the Domesday Book the Bishop of Chester held most of the land. In 1322 it was sold to John de Rale, or Ralegh, a member of the Raleigh family of Devon. The Raleighs had financial difficulties especially after the Civil War and the Holbech family bought the estate in 1684 for £8,700. It remained an estate village until 1960 when it was transferred to the National Trust.

At one time the village was self-supporting with butcher, baker, basket makers and the women weaving at home. Most of the men worked on the farms and the estate. Farnborough Hall was double the size it is now and included a brewery and laundry. Until the Second World War, The Butchers Arms was only a beer house as the 'workers did not need anything stronger' and if spirits were required for medicinal purposes the Lady of the Manor would supply them.

Dame Berry lived in a house near the village pool in the early 1800s. One Saturday the foxhounds came to Farnborough and chased the fox into the village where it jumped onto the Dame's house and down the chimney. The old lady was very annoyed at this for she had just cleaned her house and the fox brought a lot of soot with him. She locked him in and when the huntsman came would not allow him to be taken unless they paid her a shilling. This was agreed and the fox was taken to Windmill Hill and liberated.

A thrush caught by the late Henry Holbech was buried beside the gravel walk at the Hall and the following lines marked his last resting place.

> Here lies the body of a poor thrush,
> Whom death unhappily did crush,
> Before he was fledged, young Henry caught him
> And to the cage he quickly brought him
> With care and tenderness he was fed
> And now alas! poor Dicky's dead.
> And so must we frail mortals die,
> And in the dust like Dicky lie.

The parish church of St Botolph was begun in the 12th century but has been added to over the years. A north transept and spire were added in 1875. There are memorials to some of the Raleigh family and later ones to the Holbech family.

The church fete is called Farnborough Wake and is now held at Farnborough Hall on the first Saturday in July. For many years it was held on the Monday evening after Wake Sunday. If you attended church on this day you were allowed to walk along the Terrace Walk at the Hall. There is a 'Wake' pudding, something like a rich bread pudding.

The village school has now closed and the post office closed some years ago. The village hall was built after the First World War from an old army hut and still stands to provide a place for meetings and the weekly whist drives and Christmas bazaar.

🍁 FENNY COMPTON

The village lies in the shadow of the remains of an Iron Age fort on Gredenton Hill, which is part of the Burton Dassett range on the edge of the Cotswolds. Many of the houses are built in the local warm, honey-coloured ironstone, but Fenny Compton is not only pretty but is also a self-reliant working village. Fenny Compton is lucky to have a Co-op shop, part-time post office, hairdresser and a picture framer. With the closure of Farnborough and Northend schools in 1997 its school was enlarged and now has about 170 pupils. There is also a modern doctor's surgery, church, chapel, two public houses and a maintained fire station.

Two new main housing developments were built in the second half of the 1990s which, together with infilling, have provided about 70 new homes and increased the population by one third.

The Water Company, founded in 1886, is the smallest in England, supplying about 40 consumers. The water is gravity-fed from a spring in the Burton Dassett Hills. The old financial records of the company make fascinating reading. There is a bill from 1937 for mutton fat at 1s 4d and calico at 1s 4d. What for? You might wonder! In those days repairing a burst pipe entailed lighting a wood fire on site to melt mutton fat in a saucepan. Calico was then wrapped around the hole, painted with the mutton fat and allowed to set. Some of these joints are said to be holding to the present day. 'Fenny water', as it is affectionately known, is an essential ingredient for a perfect cup of tea.

🍁 FILLONGLEY

Fillongley is a neat, pleasant village in an extensive parish, situated six miles from Coventry, Nuneaton and Coleshill. It lies in a hollow, steeply bounded on the east and south by hills giving remarkable panoramic views. The name possibly comes from 'Fylle' meaning 'wild thyme' or from 'Fyllan', meaning to 'clear a forest'. The spelling of Fillongley in the Domesday Book (1086) varies from Fillonglei to Filunger. Locals suggest it is a corruption of 'Feel Lonely', something quite alien to this friendly village!

The historian, William Dugdale, writes, 'Two castles anciently stood at Fillongley'. One being the seat of the powerful De Hastings family. Early records show that a portion of land known as 'Old Fillongley' was in the possession of the Monks of Coventry at the time of the Norman Conquest. Today's inhabitants are very proud of its ancient history.

The most prominent building in the village centre is the 13th century church of St Mary and All Saints. For some years now the Anglicans and Methodists of Fillongley have merged into a happy union, and often services are shared by the Vicar and the Methodist Minister. There is a church choir, a Choral Society, a tower of bell-ringers and a team of hand-bell ringers. It is a very caring community and those attending church regularly become aware of a feeling of fellowship and of belonging to a family. A flourishing Sunday school is held in the Meeting Room built onto the church in recent years. This room also hosts numerous social occasions.

The churchyard has a ghost; an apparition of a lady wearing a long dress, has been seen 'walking through the churchyard on dark and misty evenings'. Those who have witnessed it no longer use the churchyard path as a short cut.

There are various charities in Fillongley which have their origins in the church; an Educational Charity; one providing gifts (now money) at Christmas for the aged and poor of the parish; and for many years a Bread charity which distributed bread to the needy.

An old custom in Fillongley was 'Beating the Bounds'. Members of the church, together with four boys, assembled at church on Rogation Day and after prayers proceeded to walk around the boundary of the parish, some 32 miles; the vicar meeting the procession at specified places along the route.

Another ancient custom was a market, held every Monday. Items offered for sale, such as eggs, butter, cloth, were placed on the steps of the Market Cross in the churchyard. Fees for the sale of these goods were collected by a Steward and went to the Lord of the Manor. Fillongley also held an annual fair at one time, which commenced on the eve of St John the Baptist and lasted for six days.

There is a curious tale of the huge tree, 'The Kinwalsey Elm', on the borders of Meriden, Fillongley and Hampton. It is known locally as 'Kinnesy Church', from the days when John Wesley and other divines preached beneath its spreading branches; and its trunk was used for posting notices, as if it were a church door. The tale tells of a couple caught stealing from a hen-roost on a neighbouring farm. They were tried by a local jury, condemned and 'hung on the nearest tree'. Their bodies were cut down, carried to a nearby common, cast into a hole and a stake driven through them. It seems the stake was green and took root. It grew into a tree, with branches growing only out of its sides as its head had been blunted by the mallet.

The bustling village tradesmen are mostly gone now, the black-smiths, bakers, carpenters, painters, plumbers, shoemakers, wheelwrights, stone-masons, rope-makers, maltsters and weavers; leaving only names such as 'Weavers Arms', so called from the family of weavers who once lived there, to remind us of bygone days. Those who work locally now do so in the village shops or on the farms, others travel to the factories and offices in the nearby towns.

Fillongley is well looked after for 'refreshment'; it has four public houses and a Working Men's Club. This was formed in 1890, to serve the needs of the male working population; in recent years it has been open to the 'ladies' too and it is now a very popular social meeting place. The other public houses are the

The Bell Cottages, Fillongley

Butchers Arms, and the Manor, within the village street, and the Cottage Inn set in the old lane leading to Coleshill.

The village has a post office, hairdresser, newsagent (Bed and Breakfast), a well stocked general food store, a butcher's shop and a garage; it also has its own resident policeman. Buses run through the village into Coventry and Nuneaton, and recently a popular 'free' bus service has been introduced to take village folk into nearby Bedworth for the supermarkets etc. There are two schools; one, originally the Infants School, is being converted into a community centre, with a library and rooms for social functions, where villagers can meet and chat, fostering friendships and stimulating interest in village life. The other school is still used as a place of education.

A little verse comes to mind referring to its one-time headmaster, Mr Peter Kay, a man revered rather than feared. How many remember reciting:

> 'Peter Kay is a very good man,
> He tries to teach us all he can,
> Read and write and arithmetic,

He doesn't forget to give us the stick.
When he does, he makes us dance,
Out of England into France,
Out of France and into Spain,
Over the hills and back again.'

The knightly De Hastings family who once lived here, have long ago departed, and moss creeps over their once proud castle. The visitor as he passes along the village street and sees the ancient church may recapture something of the spirit of Fillongley's antiquity; and if he is inclined to meditation as he gazes over the village to the woods and fields still there, may recall,

'Dull would he be of soul, who could believe
that the fragrance of wild thyme was unknown
to those who first gave Fillongley its name.'

🍁 FRANKTON

Frankton formed part of the land granted by Earl Leofric to Coventry Priory on its foundation in 1043. After the Dissolution of the Monasteries this manor was kept in Crown hands until 1579–80 when it was granted to Thomas Thornton and Thomas Woodcock, from whom it passed to the Temple family. In 1680 Richard Temple sold the property to Sir Theophilus Biddulph of Westcoome, Greenwich, in which family it remained until after the Second World War.

The church of St Nicholas has a 13th century tower, but is mainly 19th century work. In the church burial register is the signature of Frederick Temple, 1821–1902, who was headmaster of Rugby School and later Archbishop of Canterbury. He attended a burial here of a member of the Powlett family.

The manor, built 1662, like most manor houses created its own fish pools and these are still in use during the fishing season. The first mention of the Rectory is 1304.

71

The old school just off the street was maintained from a charity paid twice a year: Lady Day and Michaelmas. In 1878 a 'New School' was erected and remained open until the early 1940s when the children went to Bourton Village School. The inhabitants of Frankton decided that what was needed was a village hall – so a Village Hall Committee was formed, and the school converted to a hall. The village hall is now a private dwelling and entertainment is held in the Friendly Inn.

Frankton is a quiet village. Most of the houses and bungalows are occupied by professional people.

Funds were collected at the end of the First World War for the erection of a 'Memorial to the Fallen'. The position of the Memorial was left to the mothers of the fallen – a wise decision. It is placed in the interior of the church.

❧ GAYDON WITH CHADSHUNT

Gaydon is a small village with a population in the region of 300 just off what used to be the A41, now the B4100. This change occurred with the opening of the M40 just behind Gaydon Hill. The B4100 remains fairly busy especially early mornings and evenings.

The spired church of St Giles was built about 1852 in a 14th century style to replace an old chapel and the clock is a memorial to those who gave their lives in the 1914–18 war. Gaydon was fortunate in that no one was lost in the 1939–45 war. The clock has recently been restored and regilded.

The nearby hamlet of Chadshunt has its own church dating from 1312 which has been taken over by the Historic Churches Fund. Some five services per year can now be held there – one or two weddings and christenings too. Harvest Festival is celebrated by candlelight and much restoration work has been done: the six bells can now be rung after many silent years.

A very old iron clock mechanism was found in the bell tower in the 1950s during cleaning operations but no one has any knowledge of how it came to be there or that it was ever installed.

It was cleaned and found to be in perfect working order.

Until the 1970s Chadshunt Hall had a magnificent herd of pedigree Hereford cattle and could boast of having won the Supreme Championship at the Royal Show.

Chadshunt was once more important than Gaydon but by 1879 the population of the two places reversed and Gaydon became the larger of the two.

Chadshunt can claim a connection with the Battle of Edgehill in 1642, for near the boundary with Kineton there is a field known as Rupert's Headland. Here the Prince is said to have reformed his cavalry after their famous charge. They had stopped to pillage the Parliamentary baggage left in Kineton but had retreated in disorder to this field on the unexpected arrival of Roundhead reinforcements.

The Gaydon Inn has been in existence for many hundreds of years. It was an important hostelry, being the only inn on the Warwick-Banbury road for many miles. In 1789 John Smith of Culworth was caught in highway robbery on the Banbury Road at Gaydon and was locked up for the night in an upper room at the inn where he carved his name on a beam. He was taken to Warwick and tried at the Assizes and hanged that same year. The Malt Shovel is the other public house in Gaydon.

Farming has long been the main industry, but like many areas, is mostly arable. Some sheep and a few horses are still kept. One other small business is a firm supplying wooden planters, water features, pumps and the like and which earned an award for Excellence and Enterprise in 1999. Some farmland has been sold for house building and farmhouses are now private dwellings. Other infilling has also meant extra houses in the village.

Several older houses are built with Gaydon bricks made from the yellow clay found near the surface and drainpipes were made from the blue clay of the understrata. The brickyard became a County Council store but now a house stands on the site.

The one and only village shop closed a few years ago and two cottages have been built on that plot of land. There is a garage and an Esso service station on the main road but with no school, post office or general store it is now, sadly, a 'dormitory' village.

The village hall was built in 1886 and is said to be the second oldest in the country. A new floor was put in during the early 1970s and repairs and renovations undertaken over the years.

🍁 GRANDBOROUGH

The present name, Grandborough, can be traced back to about 1538. Other known variations have been Greneburgh, Raneberge, and Grendeburgh. It is thought that they all have the same meaning – Green Hill.

Set in the heart of unspoilt Warwickshire farmland, practically on the banks of the river Leam, it is a village with an assortment of cottages, houses and farms. Many of the farm buildings are constructed in traditional Warwickshire red brick but these are being interspersed by a number of more modern houses and bungalows. More recently two small developments have swelled the population.

As one approaches the village, three spires can be seen towering into the sky. One is the spire of St Peter's, the parish church, and the other two are those of Wellingtonian fir trees which seem bent on outdoing the original painting *The way to Heaven*. The church was built of stone during the 14th century and villagers are frequently engaged in fund raising activities for renovation work both to the steeple and interior of the building.

Three hundred yards away from St Peter's lies the Primitive Methodist chapel built in 1856. It was here that a local preacher, Elijah Cadman, kicked the front panel out of the pulpit whilst preaching his sermon. To quote Cadman:

'I was telling the congregation that after the devil returned his last temptation Jesus ordered him off, and gave him a kick that sent him howling through the air. My foot being in harmony with my subject, gave a kick as to send the front panel of the pulpit flying down the aisle, whereupon some of the members shouted "Glory".'

There is a commemorative plaque set in the front panel of the pulpit and a framed manuscript relating the story.

Grandborough must once have been an important place as it boasted three inns. Only one, The Shoulder of Mutton, serves its original purpose, but The Harrow at Woolscott and The Royal George remain as tastefully modernised homes.

The village school, built in 1840, no longer exists as a school but as a house. Children now have to be transported to neighbouring villages but many of the locals can remember being taught in 'the little room' and 'the big room' from the age of four or five until eleven or older. They look back fondly on the years that they spent there and many remember the motto which still remains as an inscription on the outer wall – 'Train up a child in the best way he should go, and when he is old, he will not depart from it'.

1997 saw the closure of the village shop and post office, and with its demise the loss of a place not only to shop and collect family allowance and pension, but somewhere to catch up on local news. However, the villagers have made up for this with a huge fund raising effort to double the size of the village hall.

Grandborough Village

Activities here cater for all ages and tastes – Youth Club and Young Farmers, bingo and whist, WI and a Wine Association, as well as the more traditional dances and discos for special events.

One of Grandborough's claims to fame is that it was once connected with the famous 'Match' rugby balls. Mr Harry Timms (who still has relatives in the village) worked at Gilberts in Rugby where they made the balls for many club and international matches. Even after his retirement he could be seen in his cottage doorway, stitching the balls and thus bringing world fame to Grandborough.

🍁 GREAT ALNE & KINWARTON

Great Alne and Kinwarton, which straddle the B4089 Alcester to Henley Road, are not marked on some maps, but both have much to commend them.

The river Alne bounds the two parishes on the south-eastern side and gives its name to the village of Great Alne. It was known as the 'Alwine', meaning 'clear and bright' to the Britons who lived here and even now is a haven for wildlife. It also provided the power for Great Alne Mill, mentioned in the Domesday Book, which continued to grind wheat into flour until the 1980s.

Tucked under the hill on the outskirts of Great Alne was the Rockwell Standard factory, a reminder of the evacuation of many such factories from Coventry in 1942 into country areas. Now broken up into industrial units, it stood on the site of Great Alne Hall and Park and brought considerable prosperity to the village, even if it was blamed for the few incendiary bombs which fell in the village during the Second World War.

A relatively small number of villagers today are natives. A few can tell how they saw the opening of the river bridge in 1912, accompanied by the distribution of buns and ginger beer for the children. Before that time, when conditions permitted, farm carts trundled through the ford, as they had done since Roman times, when there was a settlement here and soldiers from the garrison in Alcester guarded the crossing. Less than half a century ago, when the house known as Shawford was built on rising ground nearby, fragments of Roman pottery and a coin came to light.

Near the river too, at this point, in 1876 men brought the railway. A quaint engine known as the 'Coffee Pot', drew a few carriages back and forth between Alcester and Bearley daily until the end of the First World War. Usefully opened again for the Second World War, the line was finally closed when railways were nationalised.

The name of the only remaining hostelry, The Mother Huff Cap, which is believed to be found in no other place in the country, is explained in the following verse:

> 'Twixt Michaelmas and Martinmas
> Old dame began to brew,
> With half a pint of old malt
> And half a pint of new.
> First twenty gallons of Huff my Cap,
> Then twenty gallons worse than that,
> Then twenty gallons as amber clear,
> And then she brewed the servants' beer.'

Kinwarton and Great Alne are indissolubly joined. The two charming churches have always been under one rector. The Memorial Hall, built in memory of those from both places who served in the two wars, is a meeting place for the usual organisations. The modern day school caters for children both of Great Alne and Kinwarton, just as the old one did. This can be seen as one leaves Great Alne for Kinwarton. It was built in 1840 by the efforts of the rector, Richard Seymour, who was a frequent visitor. On the wall near the door is the ring to which he tied his horse.

Kinwarton has its special possession too. In a field near the church is a dovecote which in medieval times housed birds to augment the winter meat ration of the Lord of the Manor. There is only one other working model like this, and many visitors are attracted annually. The dovecote and the church are the only visible reminder of one of the 'lost villages of Warwickshire'.

❧ GREAT WOLFORD

Great Wolford is the first village in Warwickshire, if you enter the county from the Four Shires Stone. This large pillar stands square at the end of the road leading to the village, and once marked the ancient boundaries of Oxfordshire, Gloucestershire, Worcestershire and Warwickshire. Years ago illegal fights and bear baiting were held there – when the law arrived from one county, everyone just moved a few yards into another.

Great Wolford, with its small village green and attractive Cotswold style houses, many with gables and diamond patterned windows, has a cosy compact feel and still retains a rural peacefulness that is often lost in villages today. The similarity of many of the houses is noticeable, due to the fact that Great Wolford was part of the estate of Lord Redesdale of Batsford Park until 1924 when it was sold.

There are no shops in the village now, but there is still a lovely Cotswold pub, The Fox and Hounds, one of the oldest buildings in the village, and very popular with visitors for its excellent food. Some say that it is 13th century. There are several farms within the parish, three of them with their farmhouses and buildings in the village itself.

There is a thriving church which was rebuilt in the 19th century on the foundations of its 12th century predecessor. Not a beautiful church, some say, but with one of the best views in Warwickshire across the valley to Little Wolford and beyond – a lovely place to rest. The parish is one of seven looked after by a vicar living in Long Compton and a curate living in the vicarage in Great Wolford. They are helped in providing a service in each church nearly every week by several retired clergy.

In the past, village life was very different from today, for there were many more children, and very large families would live in the two-up-two-down tied cottages which are now modernised, extended and picturesque properties. Those who lost their jobs in the past, lost their homes, and there was always the fear of the workhouse at Chipping Norton where they earned their keep by breaking stones for the road:

When I was young and in my prime
I broke my stones by half past nine,
But now I'm old and getting grey,
It takes me all the blooming day.

Mostly the reminiscences are of happier times, playing endlessly in the fields and enjoying and relying on folk laws and country sayings to predict the weather, for instance:

When Cadly Clump wears its cap
Wolford chaps will have a drap.

Great Wolford has expanded slowly – a little infilling here and there, and a group of several new houses built in traditional style where farm buildings used to be in the village. However, the village manages to keep its rural charm, and the countryside changes little – the bluebells still bloom every spring in Wolford Woods and the snowdrops cover the churchyard as they have done for hundreds of years.

GRENDON

Grendon is an unpretentious village which can boast the best of both worlds. On the one hand, it is situated on the A5 trunk road which makes for easy access to the main motorways. However, contrastingly the moment one leaves the A5 and its traffic, one finds the leafy lanes which lead to All Saints church standing in beautiful surroundings beside the river Anker. The land was given to Henry Ferrers by William the Conqueror and the first rector was Henry De Grendon. It is a moving experience to stand on the river bridge and take in the beautiful views, where the old Norman church appears to have moulded itself into the landscape, proudly standing there since around 1250, symbolising all that is good about Grendon.

Grendon Hall, which was owned by the Chetwynd family, stood beside the church. Sadly, only the Coach House now remains, as the Hall was demolished in the 1930s, at which time it was purchased by an American who had it shipped brick by brick to his home town and restored to its former grandeur. In its heyday the Hall provided many locals with employment such as maids, gardeners etc.

Grendon was popular with royalty in this bygone age and many times in the late 1920s the late Duke of Windsor, then Prince of Wales, could be seen when visiting the home of Mr and Mrs Harry Brown at the Croft House. Mr Brown owned a string of racehorses and the Prince was often seen out riding. The jockeys lived in a house situated on the drive leading to the church and their skills were an impressive sight to behold when exercising the horses in the nearby fields. Several local girls had romantic encounters with the jockeys, culminating in at least one wedding.

The Coventry Canal, with its attendant locks in the vicinity, runs through Grendon and is dominated by a very picturesque hump-back bridge. The village school stands near the bridge set amongst green fields. It was built in 1871 and in those days all the village children attended for the whole of their school lives, leaving at the age of 13. The school closed in July 1994 and is now run privately as a nursery school. There is also a Day Special School in Spon Lane which opened in 1963 and caters for children with moderate learning difficulties.

On the A5 stands the post office and the Village Stores. There were also two bakeries founded in 1912 by the brothers, Thomas and William Gayton. The Maypole Lane Bakery is still being run by the third generation of William's family. Sadly however, the Watling Street bakery has been closed. Although there are quite a few farms employing people in Grendon today, there is no other industry.

The Methodist chapel opened in 1885 and stands at the foot of Boot Hill. The last weekend in June the Grendon Wake was held, and it always coincided with the Methodist Chapel Anniversary, the fair taking place in the field opposite the chapel. The main Wakes Day was held on the Monday attracting many people from the surrounding villages, where the music could be heard well into the early hours of the Tuesday, and many a romance blossomed at the 'Grenwake'. That weekend, the local gardeners always aimed to harvest the first new potatoes and peas for lunch on the Sunday. Sadly, the Festival did not survive the onset of the Second World War and has never been revived. Grendon did not escape the ravages of the Second World War, as in June 1940 several bombs were dropped, resulting in nine deaths. There was an Isolation Hospital which treated infectious diseases, but modern vaccinations have eliminated the need for this facility and it is now used for boarding kennels.

HALFORD

If you drive carefully along the Fosse Way through Halford you may see Reg pushing his beautiful little truck REG 1. He will be walking to the bowling green carrying on a tradition of its care spanning over 200 years. This green has been the subject of changing fortunes. There were times when it was in a sad condition, and a time when the Halford Bowling Club withdrew permission allowing the Benefit Club and friends to play there as the grass had been 'injured' soon after it had been 'returfed at some expense'. Years before 7s 6d was paid for 'two days' work amending ye benchis for ye green' and 'for stuf for ye benchis'.

The whole character of the Club has drastically altered over the years. Two hundred years ago the members were men of substance. Names recorded about that time are very familiar today. The descendants of Holbech, West, Verney, Shirley and Leigh still live on the ancestral estates. As many as seven clergymen subscribed in one year and others, for example the Rev. Abel Humphrys of Lighthorne, were hoping to be elected. Notably Fiennes Sanderson Miller Esq of Radway was also one of the select band who met together one afternoon a week. This gentleman, the son of the famous architect who was responsible for many beautiful buildings in the Midlands, may have received his unusual name as a result of his father's connection with the family at Broughton Castle. We can imagine them travelling on horseback, or maybe by carriage, from as far afield as Stoneleigh and Farnborough, those from the north having to stop as they entered the village in order to pay their toll. Others would have crossed the historic stone bridge where the Cavaliers won a victory in the Civil War. Now the players still come from other villages but are drawn from all walks of life, able to play only at weekends and during the summer evenings.

But did those eminent gentlemen really come for the sport? Or was it rather for the excellent venison from the parks of Charlecote, Ettington or Alscot, washed down with a good port, that was the attraction? At one time 74 bottles were stored in the cellar of the Club House together with 67 bottles of sherry. Perhaps the partaking of an ample dinner explains why it was necessary for the marker to put the wood into each player's hand with the bias placed at the correct angle. Our present members, believing that the game's the thing, are content with a modest tea and, later on, some refreshment at the Halford Bridge Inn. Here again is change! Our inn was formerly called The Bell!

'Observe always that everything is the result of a change', says Marcus Aurelius Antoninus. Thus the solid stone built village hall has resulted from the demise of the school. Attractive dwellings have appeared which once were derelict cottages. The beloved cobbler's shop, a good meeting place, has gone. The picturesque, though delapidated thatched building, a well known landmark, has been sacrificed on the altar of the god called motor car. The road is wider. A new bridge has been built.

And what of the Bowling Club? The old Club House with its cellar below and cockpit above is no more, replaced by a smart new pavilion beside the green from which you may now see Reg emerging, having completed his work, enabling still, though changed, the continuation of the game mentioned by Ferrars of Baddesley Clinton who, in 1575, commented on 'The Great Bowling at Hawford'.

❦ HAMPTON LUCY & CHARLECOTE

Hampton Lucy and Charlecote lie half a mile apart on either side of the Avon. They were once linked by a ford, now by bridges. Hampton Lucy is on the north of the Avon where the river makes a great loop on its way to Stratford-upon-Avon. On this side was the Forest of Arden. Charlecote is on the flat Felden south side where fertile land stretches to the Vale of the Red Horse and the Edgehills.

The lane between the villages runs alongside Charlecote Park, home of some of the most photographed deer in England; past Charlecote Water Mill, now working again after a lapse of many years and often open to the public; and over one of the earliest iron bridges in the country.

On the north-east edge of Hampton Lucy is Hampton Wood, an area of ancient woodland now in the care of the Warwickshire Nature Conservation Trust. This once formed part of the Fulbrook Castle domains purchased by Sir Thomas Lucy, who had inherited the Charlecote Estate in 1605. This Sir Thomas (the third) was said to be a friend of William Shakespeare. It was his grandfather whose deer the young Shakespeare is alleged to have poached! In the wood are earthworks, probably part of the boundary of the Lucy deer park. Hampton Wood has an Open Day in May when the spring flowers are at their most beautiful.

Since the 16th century, both villages have been bound up with the story of the Lucy family of Charlecote. The older houses, one in Charlecote and several in Hampton Lucy, are still thatched and were once Lucy estate cottages. Many were built in the local brick, the clay for which came from Brick Kiln Field near the mill. The first village schools were provided by the Lucys.

Charlecote had, once, a Norman church and Hampton Lucy a medieval church. Both churches were rebuilt in the 19th century by members of the Lucy family. St Leonard's, Charlecote, rebuilt by Mrs Mary Elizabeth Lucy in memory of her husband, stands within the parkland of Charlecote House and contains several old Lucy tombs as well as more recent family memorials. St Peter ad

Vincula, rebuilt by the first Rev John Lucy, Rector of Hampton Lucy, is one of the earliest examples of Victorian Gothic and, when seen from across the river and fields, shows clearly in its architecture the inspiration of Worcester Cathedral. From the time of King Offa to the reign of Mary Tudor the parish had belonged to the See of Worcester and was called Bishops Hampton.

Beyond the church the house called Avonside was once Hampton Lucy Grammar School which numbered among its pupils Charles Maries, the eminent Victorian botanist. Many of the Maries family are buried in the churchyard.

Charlecote House is one of the most popular National Trust properties and part of any Shakespearean pilgrimage. Almost opposite its gates is a 'tumbledown' stile also part of local history. On the Hampton Lucy side of the river a footpath leads from Sal's grave – the burial place of a local witch – towards Stratford-upon-Avon along high ground above the Avon reputed to be 'The bank whereon the wild thyme blows' (*A Midsummer Night's Dream*).

This lovely part of Warwickshire is full of natural beauty, history and legend, and must have brought pleasure to millions – though living on a tourist route has its disadvantages, when visitors ignore speed limits or park on blind corners! However, it is in a vulnerable position, liable to damage from insensitive development and if the river were to be opened up to motor-boats and commercialisation, this tranquil stretch of Shakespeare's Avon with its swans and its willows, its yellow water lilies and its purple loosestrife would be lost forever.

❦ HAMPTON ON THE HILL, HAMPTON MAGNA & BUDBROOKE

On 18th August 1642, before civil war became official with the raising of the Royalist Standard at Nottingham, an encounter between Parliamentarian and Royalist forces took place near Warwick. This was at Grove Park, Hampton on the Hill, the home of the Catholic Royalist, Robert Dormer, 1st Earl of Caernarvon.

The Dormer family built the Roman Catholic church at Hampton on the Hill, called St Charles of Borromeo, after an Archbishop of Milan. It was completed in 1819 and was a gift to the parish. The tribune and crypt are reserved for the Dormer family for all time. The statue of Mary wearing a cross and chain is thought to be the only one in England. It denotes her appearance at La Salette, South of France, at the time the church was built.

In a block of houses at the entrance to Grove Park is a building which used to be the Roman Catholic school; the cross and the shape of the windows can still be seen at the gable end. The Church of England school used to be in Old School Lane, just below the village hall (this has now been made into two separate homes). The Roman Catholic school closed in 1889 whilst the Church of England school moved from its original site to larger premises in the centre of the village. This closed in 1968 when the new school at Hampton Magna opened. For a short time the old school was an outpost of Warwick library, but this has been demolished and three houses have taken its place.

St Michael's, Budbrooke, which can trace an unbroken line of incumbents and vicars from 1273, was for many years the garrison church for the Royal Warwickshire Regiment, as their barracks were at Budbrooke.

The lectern in the church was presented by the 3rd Battalion and the Bible in the children's corner was given by the Officers Mess. The Regimental Colour, an antelope on a blue background, hangs high on the north wall close to the parish War Memorial tablet. When the Regiment finally left Budbrooke Barracks, they made another presentation to the church, this time a weather vane.

The Barracks were slowly run down and the men moved to Glen Parva in 1960. Buildings were completely dismantled and finally knocked down to make way for Hampton Magna. Ash House stands between the last row of houses built for use by Army personnel and the first of the new houses at Hampton Magna.

Keeping the links with the Regiment, the pub, once called Bout Time, was changed a few years ago, to Montgomery of Alamein. Three shops, a school taking children from 5 to 11 years, a new medical centre, a thriving community centre and a village hall at Hampton on the Hill all help to make up this 21st century village, with its roots firmly in the past.

🍁 HARBOROUGH MAGNA

This village in the Borough of Rugby, with its hamlets of Harborough Parva and Cathiron, has a population of about 420. It was mentioned in the Domesday Book, as having a priest and a mill.

The village was once self sufficient, with its own smithy, wheelwright and shops. There was work for men on the farms, but the largest source of employment was at the timber yards, owned by William Ivens. The saw mills were at Cathiron, near the canal. Here the seasoned timber was put on to barges for its journey to the factories.

Carts and massive cart horses were kept in fields and stables at Harborough Parva. The men would take their teams of horses to collect the trees from the estates. These were loaded on the carts, and secured by chains. The horses would pull the trees to Rugby station, where they were cut into smaller pieces by a huge machine, and taken to the saw mills. If the estates were too far away, the trees would be loaded on to special trains, and taken to Rugby. One tree from the Lawford Grange estate, was so big, it needed 18 horses to pull it.

Pleasure boats use the canal now, watched by fishermen. There are pleasant walks around the lanes, and these are popular for horse riding. Farming is now the main industry, there are herds of Friesian and Jersey dairy cows. Sheep, pigs, and goats are reared, also geese and free range hens.

There are many old houses. One built in the 17th century still has a wall of wattle and daub. The Old Lion originally The Golden Lion, built in the 18th century, has been restored after having a disastrous fire in July 1986.

St Mary's Nursing Home, was a maternity hospital from 1949–1983. This closed down, when the new maternity unit was opened at St Cross Hospital, Rugby, and is now a residential home for the elderly. St Mary's was built originally as an isolation hospital. In the early years, before they used a motorised ambulance, a farmer would harness his horse to an ambulance and, taking a nurse with him, would set off to collect any patients for admission.

Harborough Magna C of E first school, is in the centre of the village. It was built in 1845 as a National School.

All Saints church stands on higher ground and has a list of incumbents dating from 1305. The clock face in the tower was replaced in 1983. The new one has an unusual design, showing the symbols of the four Evangelists.

🍁 HARBURY

History in Harbury reaches back to before recorded time.

In the old quarries skeletons of plesiosaurus and marine dinosaurs have been found, over 100,000 years old, while Bronze Age cooking pots are the earliest proof of human habitation. By 500 BC the Iron Age chief Hereburgh ruled her tribe in a 'byrig' or camp, fortified by an extensive earthwork which still exists within the bounds of present day Harbury, whose modern name is a modification of the redoubtable lady's own.

The Roman Fosse Way marks one of the village boundaries and today one of the culverts the Romans built still carries away flood water in parts of the village.

The Saxons left proof of their presence in the ridge and furrow in the fields around, a recognisable result of their farming methods. Much later land was owned by the Knights Templars and is now remembered as Temple End.

Harbury is now a large village pulsating with activity and thoroughly forward looking. And yet the past has a strange way of reappearing. The Roman legions are still seen marching along the nearby Fosse Way, heading towards their ancient posting station under the hill. Men and horses are picked up in the headlights, only to dissolve as the car reaches them.

Behind the Norman church stands the old Wagstaff School founded in 1611, now a house. There, a ghostly figure in a black coat has been seen to hurry across the road and into the nearby churchyard, where he strides angrily round the church, and into the old school. Some say he was protesting against misuse of funds for the school. Others say that he only appeared when he did not approve of the headmaster. Someone even took a pot at him, and the bullet holes are still to be seen in the schoolhouse door. With the modern school at the far end of the village, he is now, presumably, out of a job. No one seems to know exactly who he was. But perhaps he lived in the cottage opposite. Certainly it has an eerie atmosphere with too many unexplained noises and objects which move themselves around, and sometimes disappear. No one ever chooses to live there for very long.

🍁 HARTSHILL

There is evidence of the development of the village of Hartshill for hundreds of years, since before the arrival of the Roman conquerors. It stands on an island of ancient rock off the range of hills overlooking the Leicestershire plains. For that reason it has attracted settlers ever since the Ice Age ended over the Midlands. The name Hardreshulle, now Hartshill, was derived from the Saxon words Heardred's Hill. Today several new housing estates have joined the village to the outer suburbs of Nuneaton and so it is hard to visualise the village of days gone by.

Travellers may notice the bus shelter on Hartshill Green which is the local memorial to the famous poet Michael Drayton who was born in Chapel Cottage in 1563. Older villagers can remember the ruins of his small thatched cottage on this Green. Through the efforts of a present-day local poet, John Sherwood, the memorial bus shelter was built in the shape of a scroll from local stone donated by the quarry owners. Sir John Betjeman came to Hartshill to dedicate the memorial and quoted lines from Michael Drayton's poem *A Fine Day:*

The poet Michael Drayton's cottage at Hartshill Green

'Clear had the day been from the dawn
All chequered was the sky
Thin clouds like scarfs of cobweb lawn
Veiled heaven's most glorious eye.'

Oldbury Grange is an interesting country mansion built around 1904 by Mr Garside Phillips, the first manager of Ansley Colliery, for his son Joseph. Joseph later became 'The Boss' at this pit and his family the leading gentry in the village. His grandson grew up to become Captain Mark Phillips, a renowned horseman winning the highest award at Badminton and the hand of the Princess Royal, then Princess Anne.

According to local legend there are one or two ghosts wandering around the village. The favourite is the Nun or The White Lady who is said to wander in Oldbury Road or Coppice Lane as it was first called, and over the Oldbury Hills. Her presence probably arises from the fact that before the Norman Conquest a small nunnery was built at Oldbury as an outpost of

Polesworth Abbey. The nuns kept bees and their hives were protected from the winds by specially built niches in a small facing wall. Until a few years ago there were always colonies of wild bees living in the thick walls of Oldbury Hall Gardens.

❧ HASELOR

Haselor has been a village from at least Saxon times, being mentioned as Haselove (a hazel bank) in Domesday Book and as having two Manors, Haselor and Upton. Haselor has a church, 12th century, half way between the two Manors, built on a hill that overlooks the countryside all round.

The Black Death visited the village in 1349 and a great many folk died, including possibly three rectors. There is a strong body of opinion that the original village was built around the church but that the villagers moved into the present part of the village to get away from the plague. There is still the base of a preaching cross just outside the churchyard.

The oldest house is probably in Walcote and is built on the cruck construction method. Haselor has a water mill (Hoo Mill) which ground corn for the Manor and is still used to press apples to make cider. The earliest reference to it is in 1559. Another cider mill can be found on display in Walcote.

The stocks in the middle of the village were last used in 1841 when boys who had trampled down a field of corn were punished. Haselor once had a workhouse which was turned into five cottages, now being one house called Little Manor. This stands by the old village green.

Cornelius Griffin (1846–67) was Haselor's most notorious vicar. He spent all his money on litigation, lived in the church to avoid arrest, but eventually ended up in Warwick Prison. There is a memorial to him and his sisters in the church.

An elm tree fell across the post office in 1916. It crashed through the thatched roof into the bedrooms. Amazingly the family only suffered scratches. The post office was closed in 1988 and the building is now a private residence.

The village school, opened in 1877 was threatened with closure in 1993 when it had 29 pupils. It was reprieved after a vigorous campaign and is now thriving with 98 pupils.

Haselor once boasted a round cottage called The Beehive which housed a very large family with only one room up and one down. Now all the old cottages have been modernised and are hard to recognise. The village pub has changed into private residences and farm buildings have been changed likewise. One of them has the old toll-gate posts as an entrance, a reminder that Haselor once had two toll gates, one at either end of the village on the main road.

❋ HURLEY

Hurley is situated 11 miles north-east of Birmingham and its name means 'a clearing in the forest' – in this case, the Forest of Arden. It is an agricultural and mining village, population 2,000, with a growing number of commuters, especially since the M42 motorway opened nearby in 1986; speed bumps have been put throughout the village. Situated on a hill over 300 feet above sea level, there are extensive views all round.

Hurley church, situated at the top of the hill, is a small wooden structure, erected about 1860 for a Dame School, to be used once a week for a church service. In 1895 a brick school was built in the playground and the wooden building became a full-time church. In the mid 1950s more school buildings were erected to accommodate the children of mining families, brought into the village to work at the newly sunk Daw Mill mine and other local mines. The new school buildings were erected on the site of St Edmund's chapel which had long since disappeared. The cross can still be seen in the churchyard along Heanley Lane.

Atherstone House, late 17th century, is brick with stone quoins. It is said that, during Cromwell's time a cannon ball went down the chimney. Until recently the cannon ball could be seen in the garden. An early Georgian moated house, Hurley Hall, once housed a magistrates court.

The Holly Bush Inn, which used to have steps up to its front door, overlooked the Bull Ring where the village stocks were sited. Opposite The Holly Bush were some very old cottages with wattle and daub walls and dormer windows. One of these was called the Nutshell and, although very tiny, was the home of a very large family. On the right, going down Knowle Hill, was the blacksmith's forge. It is now a garage.

Dexter colliery was sunk on the south side of the village in the mid 1920s. It was demolished in 1987. The coal from Dexter was taken along a specially constructed overground track to Kingsbury colliery to be screened, and no spoil was allowed to be tipped on Dexter colliery site. This track has also gone.

On the outskirts of the village, where a brook flows through a spinney to the river Tame at Kingsbury, is the site of an old paper mill.

Hurley Common is a small hamlet one mile north of Hurley village. It has 30 or so houses and two public houses, The White Hart and The Anchor. Hurley and Hurley Common are well served by shops, clubs and public houses. There are a dozen or so farms surrounding the village and several small light industries.

The villages surrounding Hurley have many interesting features. Baxterley has a lovely stone church with a rare 12th century wooden crozier head, the oldest piece of church equipment in Warwickshire. The churchyard is ablaze with wild daffodils in the spring. Merevale church has many interesting antiquities. Merevale Hall and Merevale Abbey are occasionally on view to the public. Bentley has an interesting public house called The Horse and Jockey which, other than electricity, has never been modernised. Its sign shows the present Sir William Dugdale jumping a fence in the Grand National in the 1950s.

🍁 Ilmington

Ilmington, a village of approximately 600 inhabitants, bordering the Cotswolds and lying on the edge of a fertile farming valley, derives its name from 'the elm grown hill'. Evidence of the earliest settlers is thought to date from around 2500 BC.

Four farms provide limited employment but most people commute to nearby towns.

The first Christmas broadcast by George V, in 1934, was introduced by Walton Handy, the village shepherd and relayed to the world from Ilmington Manor, a fine Elizabethan house, once owned by the De Montford family. There are many old houses built from stone quarried in the parish until the 1920s. Crab Mill, an attractive house, was the home of Lady Borwick (of Borwick Baking Powder), who was the benefactress of the maternity ward at the Ellen Badger Hospital, at Shipston. Professor Dorothy Hodgkin, a 1964 Nobel Prize Winner (the first woman since Florence Nightingale) lived at Crab Mill.

E. P. Wilson, jockey and trainer of the Grand National winner in 1884 and 1885, lived in Ilmington and trained horses over the downs, where nearby is a Roman burial ground and a clearly visible Roman road, said to have been a pig drovers route through to Wales.

There are two public houses in the village – The Red Lion, where the Court Baron met prior to Land Enclosure and The Howard Arms. The seat of the famous Howard family is at Foxcote, a nearby hamlet.

Ilmington has a chalybeate spring which was for many years renowned for its medicinal powers. Another famous watering place, Wells Close, had its own little house in the fields, where people could stay to take the waters.

The remains of a tramway, once the main form of transport to the village, can still be seen.

The church retains its fine Norman arches and the Roman Catholic church was used as a school until 1931. The Methodist chapel is used for weekly worship.

Ilmington still has a general store, post office, school, hurdlemaker, and orchards, but sadly has lost its blacksmith, baker and other craftsmen. The greatest change has been the conversion of the beautiful old stone barns into dwelling-houses.

93

🍁 KENILWORTH

Although the number of houses in Kenilworth has increased during the past few years, the pleasant atmosphere of a community which is in close proximity to city, country and university still exists. Visitors come to enjoy glimpses of history mingled with good shopping areas and leisure facilities.

Kenilworth's history can be studied through the church of St Nicholas which has a beautiful Norman doorway which was originally part of the Abbey; the monastic ruins in the Abbey Fields, including the small museum open in the Abbey Barn on summer Sunday afternoons; and the castle, founded about 1120 and eventually destroyed by Oliver Cromwell.

In 1266 Kenilworth Castle endured the longest siege in English history. A parliament at Kenilworth appointed the commissioners who drew up the terms of surrender for the rebels.

Land called Parliament Piece was given to the Open Spaces Society in 1987 by the landowner, Miss Martin. Kenilworth Common is a good place for walking, as are Crackley Woods and the 80 miles of footpaths that have been made readily accessible by the work of the Kenilworth Footpath Preservation Group. Plans are in hand for the possible introduction of a Millennium Heritage Trail which will link the site of the Castle, the Abbey and the Barn museum in Abbey Fields and the ancient parish church of St Nicholas. It is very much hoped that Kenilworth will be once again connected to the national rail network following the construction of a proposed new railway station in the town during 2000/2001.

At the beginning of the 20th century tanning and comb making were local industries but today many people are employed in Coventry, Leamington Spa or Birmingham.

🍁 KINETON

Kineton has been established for many centuries. Royal residence gave the village the name of Kington, which is mentioned in the

Domesday Book. In feudal times everyone depended on the gentry for their living. Even at the turn of the 20th century the gentry insisted that boys raised their hats and bowed to them while the girls curtsied. The children would go miles out of their way to get out of doing it.

During the 19th century, up to 1890, a cattle market was held in the village Market Square on Tuesdays. The mop fair still comes to the Market Square every year around the 4th October.

There are three public houses in the village, two dating back to the 17th century. Up to 30 years ago there was a fourth public house called The Rose and Crown, dated 1665, which was in the Market Square but that closed down and became a private dwelling.

During the Second World War Kineton was used as a transit camp, with Polish and Czechoslovakian soldiers stationed here. Later soldiers from the Pioneer Corps and REME were stationed in the village. At one time at least the area which is now called Park Piece was covered with large tents.

In 1958 Kineton High School was opened. Children aged 11 and over attended the school and buses were laid on to bring in children from the neighbouring villages. During this time many new housing estates were built, namely St Peters Road, Castle Road and Green Farm Estate.

🍁 KINGSBURY

There cannot be many villages in Warwickshire – or in the country for that matter – which can boast a sports hall, youth centre, health centre, swimming pool, 12th century church, the remains of a fortified manor house and a school founded in 1686.

Mercia was the principal Saxon kingdom when Offa became king. Tamworth was its capital and the countryside around became the king's hunting ground. A 'bury' (or fortified house) for the king was established on a bluff overlooking the river Tame. But today mention of Kingsbury conjures up pictures of coalmines, gravel pits, oil terminals, a rifle range and the Water

Park. Certainly for the first half of the 20th century, the village economy revolved around the coalmines of nearby Piccadilly and Hurley, and agriculture. However, since the end of the Second World War no fewer than four housing developments have transformed the community. Less than 140 years ago Kingsbury comprised the vicarage, school, mill, four farms, nine shops or public buildings and 17 private residences. The village was then quite self-sufficient and few owned their own houses or their businesses. The major landowner was the then Prime Minister, Sir Robert Peel.

Nowadays the majority of houses are owner-occupied and people commute to Birmingham, Coventry or Tamworth – or beyond. The pits are closed and only a few new industries have replaced them locally. Kingsbury has, however, managed to retain many essential village characteristics, much of the community still shows dedication to either the parish church or the Methodist church and many organisations stem from them.

Kingsbury's association with the famous goes back into the 'romantic' Middle Ages when two feuding families, the Bracebridges and the Ardens, experienced a true-life Romeo and Juliet love-affair. Alice Bracebridge from Kingsbury Hall married – against the wishes of both families – John Arden of Park Hall. John's brother's grand-daughter was Mary Arden, mother of William Shakespeare.

Older villagers remember the frequent floods when the river would rise and spread over the flood plain between Kingsbury and the nearby hamlet of Bodymoor Heath. This didn't stop children coming to school across muddy fields and over the 'planks' – a raised footway which still is in everyday use. Indeed, it is one of the features of the 650 acre Water Park developed from sand and gravel workings. More than 180,000 visitors a year are recorded and they can enjoy fishing in some 19 pools, sailing, watersports of all descriptions, horse riding and caravanning. One primary function of the Park is to preserve wildlife and a nature reserve provides hides for bird watchers.

Schooling in Kingsbury can be said to have started as early as 1637. In 1650 William Dugdale, the antiquarian, founded a school using the Bracebridge Chapel of the parish church. In 1686, Thomas Coton, a wealthy landowner, provided in his will for a school and a schoolmaster's house in Church Lane. That house, now a private residence, received a Commendation and Civic Award following its restoration. Now, the village has three fine schools, all sharing a central position.

❧ LADBROKE

The small village of Ladbroke is situated 2 miles south of Southam and 12 miles north of Banbury. Since it was by-passed in 1986 it has become a truly rural village.

The village of Ladbroc is mentioned in the Domesday Book. The village then had a population of 252 which is very similar to the present day population.

When asked 'where do you live?' and given the answer 'Ladbroke', the usual comment made is 'I thought that was a bookmakers'. The connection is that in the early 1900s Ladbroke House was occupied by W. H. Schwind. He was very interested in horse racing and is reputed to have had a very good eye for a horse.

When his reputation began to get well known he found it increasingly difficult to get good odds especially if it was known that he was betting. He found a solution to the problem, which involved placing bets by telegram just before a race.

This practice resulted in one bookmaker being unable to meet his obligations to Schwind. Schwind and his partners met the owners of the bookmakers from Southampton Row in London at Ladbroke and agreed to take the firm over, but as part of taking it over, the name was changed to Ladbrokes.

One of Ladbroke's other claims to fame is its connection with the Ladbroke Continental Car Group. This firm was started in the village by Mr Graham Hudson.

Ladbroke church dates back to the 13th century and was totally renovated in 1876 by the famous architect Sir Gilbert Scott. The very beautiful church has in its possession a unique set of communion plate presented by Alice, Duchess of Dudley in the late 17th century.

One of the other landmarks in Ladbroke is Ladbroke Hall. This is an imposing building set in its own lavish grounds. It was once the home of Lord Rootes, the famous car manufacturer and it later became a girls boarding school. Legend has it that there is in existence a ghost known as the 'Lady in Black' who wanders around in the dead of night. In the early 1970s the Hall was one of the first country houses to be converted into self-contained properties.

🍁 LAPWORTH

The village of Lapworth grew out of the Forest of Arden, and this determined its widely scattered dwellings, successors to the isolated farmsteads in forest clearings. It lies in the triangle formed by the two major roads from Birmingham to Stratford-upon-Avon and Warwick. The M40 traverses east to west across the parish. The oldest part of Lapworth is where St Mary's church is, but the main population live in the Station Lane area which was once known as Kingswood.

There are many examples of fine old buildings, namely 15th and 16th century farmhouses, manor houses and barns. The church of St Mary the Virgin dates back to the 12th century. There has been a church on the site for at least 800 years. The advowson of St Mary's has been in the hands of the scholars of Merton College, Oxford for over 700 years. Over the centuries many of the College graduates have occupied the office of Rector of the parish.

The old school house adjacent to the church, was built in 1828, but a school was run from a cottage which stood nearby from as early as 1783. The old school is now used for church receptions and similar events.

A new junior school was built in 1990 in Station Lane, the main population area of Lapworth. The school accommodates 120 children.

Kingswood Junction Lock, Lapworth

The canal plays an important role in the life of the village. The Stratford-upon-Avon and Grand Union canals converge there. The reservoir attracts many fishermen, and colourful narrow boats provide a holiday atmosphere. A shady car park in the spinney adjoining a picnic site with barbecues attracts many people. Walkers often meet here to walk the miles of footpaths throughout Lapworth. Three attractive country pubs, The Boot, Punchbowl and Navigation provide good fare for locals and visitors.

The village hall's design reflects the barrel-roof cottage beside the canal. This is a very busy venue, something on every night! A well equipped building for all sorts of activities, and the many village societies.

🍁 LEAMINGTON HASTINGS

The parish of Leamington Hastings, anciently called Lunstone or Laminstone, was once described as 'The Town of the Hastangs on the Muddy River', taking its name from the river Leame and the family of Hastang. It includes three other hamlets – Hill, Broadwell and Kites Hardwick – and several farms, and in total covers some 3,244 acres.

In 1086 it was owned by Hasculf Musand and passed through the Hastang family, the Wheeler family and the Sitwell family, who in the early 1900s sold it off portion by portion.

The hamlet of Leamington Hastings has increased in population but in addition to the church there is a vicarage, a manor house, and almshouses which consist of eight flats. There was a church in the time of Edward the Confessor probably attached to some monastery. There is no history of it, but the earliest part of the present All Saints' church is the south arcade dating from the 13th century. In addition to church services, regular concerts are given by famous musicians, when the church is filled to capacity.

The hamlet of Hill, anciently called Hulle, derives its name from the higher ground on which it stands. It belonged to the monks of Abingdon in the time of the Conqueror and the whole estate of Hill was purchased by Robert de Hastang. In 1839 a school was built by the Rev Harvey Wilmot Sitwell at his own expense, and a dwelling house for the headmaster was built in 1844. The school was for boys and girls to the age of 14 years. This was replaced when a new school opened in November 1961, and the inscription 'Train up a child in the way it should go and when he is old he will not depart from it' was transferred from over the old school door and placed in the wall at the new school entrance. Today at the age of seven years children are transferred to Dunchurch or a similar junior school, and a nursery section has been added. The School House was sold in 1986 and is now privately owned.

The parish hall stands in just over an acre in Hill and was built in 1930. Adjoining the hall there is now a tennis court and a four-rink bowling green.

Broadwell hamlet also includes four houses near Stockton Station, which is now closed, and takes its name from a spring which always maintains an abundance of water. Broadwell House (Farm) was built by Mr Robert Sitwell. A plot of ground known as Broadwell Green was conveyed by Mr H.W. Sitwell in 1939 to trustees 'for preservation as an open space or for any use beneficial to agriculture'.

There were a number of allotments in the centre of Broadwell but sadly these are no more and dwellings have been built in their place. The shop is now closed but the post office remains open. The Victory Hall, once used as a reading room and now a small hall for functions, has been tastefully renovated.

The first Norman chapel was built on land at Broadwell House but was pulled down because of the likelihood that it might become a Nonconformist meeting house. In 1871 a Wesleyan chapel was built on the present site, and on 6th October 1912 the extended building was opened by Mr George Thomas MP (later known as Lord Tonypandy).

The Church of the Good Shepherd, originally known as Broadwell Mission Room, was conveyed in 1925 to the Diocesan Trustees and the Church Council of Leamington Hastings as

Administrative Trustees. Services are still held regularly but as the vicar of Leamington Hastings now has to serve five parishes, services have to be shared.

Broadwell Flower Show is held annually in September, when flowers, vegetables, cookery and crafts are entered for competition – this replaced the Wake of the earlier days of the 20th century. A Spring Show on a smaller scale is held in April.

The small hamlet of Kites Hardwick has the A426 passing through it. In 1236 William de Herdwick had possessions here. A public house called the Lamb was closed prior to 1887, an off-licence also closed, and the Primitive Methodist chapel no longer exists. The manor house still stands but with extensive alterations which enable more than one family to live there.

One of the charities that still exist in the parish is the Consolidated Charity, for the upkeep of the almshouses and for persons in need in the parish. The other is the Leamington Hastings School Poor's Land Trust, which offers at least two years financial assistance with education for young people who are resident in the parish and educated within the State system.

Farming has changed dramatically in the parish. After 1945 many parishioners still worked on the land and all farmers had a milking herd. At present there is only one milking herd, farms have decreased in number and the land is now worked by the remaining farmers. Some families can claim to have lived in the parish for generations, others are newcomers, but the various parish organisations work to draw the whole community together.

❧ LEEK WOOTTON

Even before its mention in the Domesday Book, 1086, the 'wooded hamlet' as its Anglo-Saxon name implies, existed. The charm of Leek Wootton lies in its compact development over recent years – careful infilling but no ugly sprawl into the surrounding woods and farmlands.

The settlement of 33 families has now grown to over 1,000

residents, and it lies between the castled towns of Warwick and Kenilworth. The main road linking these two good shopping centres (and with a 'bus service too!) carves a line through the village. On the eastern side of the road are the village school, residential estate, Ted Edgar's Ranch House and stables, the Hill Wootton hamlet and farmlands dipping down to the river Avon. Spread along the western side of Warwick Road are the church, post office/shop, The Anchor public house, several large old houses and farms, a small housing estate, and Woodcote Hall, now the Warwickshire Police Headquarters. There is a new school opposite the entrance to the golf club.

A nearby historic monument, hidden in woods high on Blacklow Hill, is a memorial to Piers Gaveston, favourite of Edward II, whose stone cross bears the chilling words – 'Beneath the hollow of this rock, on July 3rd 1312, was beheaded by Barons lawless as himself Piers Gaveston, Earl of Cornwall. A hated minion of a hated king, an instance of misrule.' Well worth a gentle climb, and rewarded in February with a carpet of snowdrops. Another favourite walk is from Guyscliffe, once a mill – where the Avon can be crossed, and up to the unspoilt hamlet and church of Old Milverton.

Between Woodcote and the school lies the Memorial Recreation Ground, with its splendid rural view across to St John's spire at Kenilworth. Amongst other activities, cricket is devotedly played here, and the well-mown grass is kept in perfect condition by Sports Club volunteers. Their club house was rebuilt in 1998/99. At one corner is the Working Men's Club and the third timber building is the village hall.

On a rising bank above the road stands the church of All Saints, stone built, and replacing an earlier one which was pulled down in 1789; but a church has stood near there since 1122. In the churchyard were buried two stragglers from the Battle of Edgehill. On the grass lies an old Norman font. Lime trees cast their shade and scent over the paths, and for these we can thank the 77 parishioners of 1844 who each planted one! The old bells in the tower are rung, and the fifth and oldest was the work of one Johannes de Stafford in the 14th century. This bell is now wired to the church clock, so the chimes that ring across the meadows could have been heard 600 years ago!

Leek Wootton is the fortunate beneficiary of a charity dating back to 1668, and this is administered as a small but welcome 'bonus' to the 'poor of the Parish' at Christmas. The same benefactor, the Duchess of Dudley, Lady Alice, also presented the beautiful communion plate of silver gilt, to the church of All Saints, and in thanksgiving her name is always remembered in church every Whit Sunday.

🍁 LILLINGTON

One of the lesser-known distinctions which England can claim is that it has undergone a successful heart transplant – and it took place at Lillington on the outskirts of Leamington Spa. The exact heart of England – if one discounts other neighbouring claimants to the honour – is at the junction of Lillington Avenue and Lillington Road, a hallowed spot marked for centuries by a venerable tree known appropriately as the Midland Oak.

In 1966 with this noble landmark suffering from old age, and the adjacent traffic artery needing widening, England's 'heart transplant' took place. The ancient oak was removed and one of its progeny planted in its place nearby to perpetuate the role of marking the centre of England. Thus is Lillington's principal claim to fame.

The first element of the village's name is derived from 'Lilla', an Anglo-Saxon thegn of Eadwine. The second element, 'tun', signifies a farmstead, so Lillington was Lilla's farm.

Indeed, with only 16 adult inhabitants in 1086, it has been mainly a farming community right up to the 20th century, when it was united with Leamington Spa. Even today the occasional farm building can still be recognised, part of one group near the church having been converted into garage premises.

From the evidence of the parish records, it would seem that the village escaped the worst ravages of the plague. The 1801 census showed a population of 178, which had increased to over 2,000

104

by 1931. Today, the figure has grown almost unbelievably to almost 20,000, with many acres of the parish now covered with council and private housing developments.

The first evidence of a parish church is from the records of Kenilworth Priory, when William de Kilkenny was made vicar of Lillington in 1252. The oldest part of the building, which is dedicated to St Mary Magdalene, is the south wall of the chancel, which is of Norman origin. However, the most interesting part of the structure is the tower which was built in the 15th century. Among its eight bells is one dated as early as 1480, while two others date from 1625 and 1675. It is an intriguing thought that a bell which Lillington folk hear rung each week, was ringing out over the same parish before Christopher Columbus discovered America.

The most noteworthy epitaph in the churchyard, and just still legible, is that to the memory of one William Treen, who died on 3rd February 1810, aged 77:

> 'I poorly liv'd and poorly dy'd
> Poorly buried and no one cry'd.'

He was known as 'Old Billy Treen, the miserd'. He is said to have been a road-scraper who existed miserably by begging potato peelings and turnips from the farmers. When he died, however, it was discovered that he had amassed a secret fortune.

There are now very few old buildings left, and the picturesque thatched and timber-framed cottages which graced Cubbington Road until the late 1960s, one of which was once old Billy Treen's home, are now no more than a nostalgic memory in the minds of older inhabitants. The handsome stone-built Manor House, near the church, has lost most of its land to housing developments, while the former 19th century home of the Unett family, Castel Froma, is now used as a home for the disabled.

It is all a far cry from Lilla's farmstead, and Lillington can certainly not count itself among Warwickshire's most eye-catching villages. But at least it can proudly say it marks the vibrant heart of all England.

🍁 LITTLE WOLFORD

Little Wolford is an unspoilt hamlet spreading along a narrow ridge in the Warwickshire fringes of the Cotswolds. The little cluster of houses and the narrow green make a village so small that many drive through without realising that they have been here. From the village the views are tremendous, over to Brailes Hill in the east, and ten miles to Broadway Tower in the west.

Of the 35 houses in the village, mainly built in Cotswold stone, the oldest and most notable is the Manor, dating from the 15th century, an L-shaped house still with its great hall. For about a hundred years this fell into disrepair, and became three cottages while the hall was used as a school, chapel and meeting place. Since its restoration in the 1930s the manor has been a most attractive private house, and its hall is still a focal point in the village as the present owners hold many fundraising activities for local charities. The restoration has not spoiled the stains on the solar stairs, reputed to be bloodstains from after the Battle of Edgehill in 1642.

Nine farmhouses lie in the parish, all originally part of the Weston Estate, as was the village. Only two are now true farmhouses. One of the others had an interesting existence in the Second World War when actors from the Old Vic Company were evacuated there and provided much amusement for the village. One farmhouse has been separated from its barns and the inevitable conversion into houses has taken place – just as some cottages have been amalgamated to make larger houses. People say that a witch used to live in one cottage in the village – perhaps true, as a devil stone was found over the back door there during modernisation.

Just on the edge of the village, a tiny lodge designed by Blore, the architect of Buckingham Palace and the long-gone Weston House, has stone angels on each corner and a stone devil over the back door. Stone carvings also decorate the two remaining fountains which used to be the main water supply in the village. The larger fountain has a very jumbled coat of arms, and a fine lion's head for the water spout.

Round the village in many grass fields lie reminders of the past – a long past, since Wolford was mentioned in the Domesday Book. Ridge and furrow from medieval farming still remains, as does the rough ground where the brickyard was, and the line of the old mill stream. Hard to find is the old Glyde Well whose water was said to hold healing properties for sick eyes and ears.

🍁 LONG COMPTON

South of Stratford-upon-Avon and deep into some of the loveliest countryside which England can boast, lies the village of Long Compton. Through the village runs the A3400, a road much used by tourists.

As its name implies, it is a very long village, and about half way along its street, surrounded by picturesque cottages in colourful gardens, stands the large church of St Peter and St Paul. Most of the building dates from the 13th century, but there was a much earlier church, possibly with a thatched roof. But what the passing motorist usually notices is the handsome lychgate. In fact this lychgate was a cottage dating from about 1600, with the lower storey removed, partly half timbered with brick infilling. The building was purchased in the 1950s by Mr Latham, a local builder, who restored and reroofed it. In 1964, after Mr Latham's death, his widow handed over the lychgate to the church as a memorial to her husband, and it is now the main entrance to the churchyard.

From a studio in Long Compton, Donald Brooke, an artist in stained glass, sent out his work far and wide.

An earlier example of village craftsmanship was the King's Stone Printing Press, set up in 1922 by the Rev William Manton. A number of books were printed, and during the General Strike of 1926 the Press published the *Long Compton Wireless News*, distributed by drivers throughout Britain.

This printing press derived its name from the King's Stone, one of the Rollright Stones which can be reached by following the A3400 up a long hill out of Long Compton. On one side of the road stands the solitary King's Stone, and on the other side are two groups of stones, the Whispering Knights and the Circle. This is the best preserved stone circle in the Midlands, visited by many people every year who come to gaze, to count the stones (very confusing!) and to relate old legends and evil deeds. The truth no one knows. Much has been written about the Stones but the mystery is not solved.

Tradition tells how a king set out to conquer England, and as he came up the hill from Great Rollright he was halted by a witch who told him to take seven long strides and then –

> 'If Long Compton thou canst see
> King of England thou shalt be.'

The king eagerly strode out, but as he took the seventh stride he saw not Long Compton but a long mound of earth which still remains. Said the witch –

> 'As Long Compton thou canst not see
> King of England thou shalt not be.
> Rise up stick, and stand still, stone,
> For King of England thou shalt be none.
> Thou and they men hoarstones shalt be,
> And I shall be an eldern tree.'

So the king became a standing stone, and his followers on the other side of the road likewise became monoliths.

🍁 LONG ITCHINGTON

'Oh yes, that's the village with the pond' – the tree-fringed pool, now home to a family of swans, is a well known landmark on the busy road from Coventry to Oxford. Older villagers call it the 'Pit', which it was. When marl was dug out to cover the light sandy soil, water drained in and filled the pit.

Long Itchington takes it's name from the river which flows through, and sometimes into, the village. Now the river Itchen, in

Saxon times it was the Icetone. Speculation suggests associations with Boadicea, Queen of the Iceni. From the Domesday Book we learn that the land was given to Cristina, a Saxon princess and great-niece of Edward the Confessor, by William the Conqueror, probably to ensure her support. It seems to have been a prosperous holding, worth twenty times as much as the Birmingham of that day. Nothing remains of those times, unless you count the stained glass roundel window in the church which commemorates the birth, in 1008, of Wulfstan, a pious little boy who grew up to be Bishop of Worcester. His piety and life of good works was recognised when, in 1203, he became St Wulfstan.

From the pond can be seen some of the buildings which reflect the long history of the village. Opposite modern housing developments and new buildings occupied by light industries is Tudor House. Built in the late 16th century as an inn, it has changed over the centuries and its use has been varied until it became a home. Perhaps its most famous occupiers were the Sitwell family. There are other fine old brick and half-timbered

Long Itchington

buildings in Long Itchington, but when Queen Elizabeth I rested in the village on her journey to Kenilworth in 1575, none was fine enough to accommodate a queen and her entourage so Robert Dudley, who had bought the manor in 1571, grudgingly erected 'a tent, which for number and shift of large and goodly rooms, might be comparable with a beautiful palace'.

The next royal progress was not so jolly. Because of its location, close to main routes through the Midlands, 17th century villagers from Long Itchington may have seen Royalists and Parliamentarians marching to draw up battle lines at the start of the Civil War. We know that skirmishes took place as cannonballs have been found.

The oldest building in the village is the church. It has undergone many changes over the years but none more dramatic than in 1762. The spire was struck by lightning, never to be replaced. Inside the church a collection of boards sets out the provisions for various charities. On St Thomas's Day one of these charities provides money for bread for the needy, known locally as 'Tommy Bread'. In the 1860s, work was done on the roof, requiring scaffolding, ropes and pulleys. This proved too much for someone. One morning, a passer-by on his way to church was stopped in his tracks. There on the roof stood a very bemused donkey.

The village is expanding but in spite of all the changes, the pond remains a meeting point and focus of village life. Much has happened around the pond. One Sunday night in 1910 a travelling preacher had delivered his sermon and was waiting at the pond for his carriage to pick him up. It began to rain as he sheltered under a tree. A blinding flash struck the tree and killed the minister. The tree was cut down and the stump became a useful seat.

At the end of the First World War, a German howitzer gun was to be displayed on the green as a war memorial. This caused some resentment so no one was surprised when the offending monument was somehow tipped into the pond, where it remained for many years until it was retrieved to be used in some other form in a new war. A more fitting memorial, if such it can be called, came with the opening, in 1967, of Galanes House for aged and incapacitated ex-servicemen. The British Legion obviously thought that Long Itchington was the type of friendly, caring community that would welcome these men.

This, then, is Long Itchington, 'a village somewhat scattered in groups of dwellings, a parish large in acreage, a community backed by tradition'.

🍁 LONG LAWFORD

When William the Conqueror compiled the Domesday Book in 1086 the village was called Leileford and held by Geoffrey de Wirce, who in 1077 founded a small priory of Benedictine monks at what was later Monks Kirby. The abbey was bequeathed to the monks of Pipewell in 1160, who were Lords of the Manor for over 400 years.

By 1332 Leileford had become Longa Lalleford and was the largest settlement in the whole district. When Henry VIII abolished the monastery in 1542 the Grange of Long Lawford and other lands were granted to Edward Boughton. Lawford Hall, the home of the Boughtons, dominated the life of the village for the next two centuries, until the murder there in 1780 of Sir Theodosius, the last male heir of the Boughtons. The hall was sold to the Caldecott family, who pulled it down as 'a thing accursed' and built Holbrook Grange on the opposite side of the river and much closer to the village.

The church of St John was built in 1839 by John Caldecott as a Chapel of Ease to Newbold church and was intended mainly for the use of the servants from Holbrook Grange. The furnishings are quite rare as the pews, pulpit and the reading desk are the original ones installed by John Caldecott and have hardly changed. Unfortunately, the church has been declared redundant as it is unsafe. This is due to architectural faults and faults in the foundations which occurred at the time of building. In fact a public meeting was held in the village in 1880 as it was realised even then that the building was unsafe, but the Caldecott family would not spend any further money on it. Services are now held in the adjacent Church Hall. The older part of the churchyard has been designated as a Nature Conservation Area, and a great deal of work by the Friends of St John's Churchyard led to the award of first prize in the Warwickshire Village Ventures Competition in 1997.

The Church Hall next door was built in 1939 on land given by Herbert Kay, headmaster of the village school for many years. The bricks of the hall bear the initials of the Sunday School children and others who each bought a brick to help build the hall.

The village has changed since those times, although many old buildings remain. Among these is the Saracens Head, now much modernised, but where in the 1800s some of the council meetings were conducted. Another building in Main Street, now a house, was the village bakery. It was in the hands of the Garratt family for hundreds of years and was where the villagers brought their Sunday dinners to be cooked by the baker for one penny. The Yorkshire pudding was taken along in a jug, to be put in at 12 o'clock. Most people kept a pig and when it was killed, brought pies and faggots in a wheelbarrow to the baker for cooking in his large ovens. Among the pies was one 'Boney Pie', made of the backbone of the pig.

It was here in the bakery that Captain Caldecott lodged with the Garratts for 30 years after leaving the Grange, when he disagreed with his sister over dressing for dinner. Born in 1836 in India he was a fierce looking but kindly man, who insisted on being addressed as Captain. His clothes were those worn by a country squire of 60 years earlier, and he wore a hat with safety pins round the brim to keep off the flies.

The old school has long since been closed and a modern one built, more suitable for today's needs and the expanding population, but it is good to see that the old school has not been pulled down but still retains some of its character as houses.

Now more and more houses are being built, but the centre still has a lot of the old buildings and the feel of a village.

🍁 LONG MARSTON

When the county boundaries were revised in 1931 Long Marston was transferred from Gloucestershire to Warwickshire. It lies some six miles south-west of Stratford-upon-Avon, where it also borders Worcestershire. The village was known as Dry Marston or Marston Sicca (both the Parish and Church Councils are still known by this name).

The first written evidence of a settlement was in 1043 when Earl Leofric granted Long Marston to the monks of Coventry on condition that a church was built there. The main industry of those days was agriculture with the inhabitants working for the monks, who were the Lords of the Manor. The people owned no property nor were they entitled to any wage, but were fed, clothed and housed by the monks.

Some 200 years later the 'Manor' was sold to the Abbey of Winchcombe for 1,130 marks (£753.33). It seems likely that it was they who built the parish church of St James the Great in the middle of the 14th century. Although it has been restored and altered since then it has an interesting oak-braced belfry, a Jacobean pulpit and a 17th century brass plaque to Samuel Burton, Archdeacon of Gloucester. It is still in the Diocese of Gloucester.

In 1539 came the Dissolution of the Monasteries – the Abbey of Winchcombe ceased to exist and the Crown took possession. In 1566 Queen Elizabeth I granted the Lordship and the Manor of Long Marston to Robert, Earl of Leicester, but he did not remain in possession long. In 1577 John Kecke and John Tomes, two yeomen, bought the land and buildings of the Manor. The Earl of Leicester retained the Lordship of the Manor until about 1602 when it was sold to Edward Sheldon, one of a well known Warwickshire family. The Sheldons, at intervals, held a court in the village, presumably at Court Farm. The three principal families of the time were Tomes, Kecke and Cooper. When John Cooper died in 1643 he left £300 for the erection and maintenance of a free school for boys from Long Marston and neighbouring parishes. The Grammar School was closed by Gloucestershire Local Education Authority in 1910, having served the educational needs of the village for some 260 years. John Cooper's money is still distributed by trustees in grants for educational purposes. The Tomes family were associated with the village until the sale of King's Lodge (formerly the Manor House) in 1976. It was here, in 1651, that Charles II stayed for one night, after his disastrous defeat at the Battle of Worcester; travelling as Will Jackson, a servant of Miss Jane Lane.

Although known in Shakespeare's rhyme as 'Dancing Marston', the village no longer has a Morris dancing team. In addition to the parish church, there is a Methodist chapel, village hall and the Mason's Arms Inn.

The airfield, which was constructed in 1940, is now used for motor sports, Sunday markets and car boot sales, light aircraft and microlight flying. The army camp, after being a Royal Engineer Stores Depot from 1940 to 1999, awaits further developments!

The Greenway is nearly five miles of what was the old railway line, running from Stratford-upon-Avon to Long Marston. It is open to walkers, cyclists and horse-riders (Milcote to Long Marston only). The Heart of England Way crosses the Greenway in Long Marston.

With the recent closure of the garage and village stores/post office, to make way for large executive type dwellings, one wonders what the future holds in store for this once agricultural community.

🍁 LOXLEY

Loxley is a small community. There are some outlying houses and farms, but the huddle of houses on the hillside forms the main part of the village.

During the 20 years prior to 1990 very few physical changes took place in Loxley. Few houses were built due to the fact that the village was a non-development area. However, during the last decade this has changed. Nine new houses have filled a gap in the affordable rental market and three other sites are being developed. Consequently when all developments are completed the village will have grown by 51 dwellings and will be half as big again as it was ten years ago.

When newly-weds come out of the church, they find the church gate festooned and tied with trails of ivy. It is the groom's job to open the gate. If he performs this task (his first as a newly married man), without using a knife, legend has it that the couple will have a long and happy married life! The church is named for St Nicholas. It stands on foundations which are amongst the oldest in the country. The site was given to the Cathedral Church of Worcester by Offa, King of Mercia in AD 760. There are several ancient ecclesiastical relics housed in the church. During the spring, the churchyard (in which, reputedly, casualties from the Battle of Edgehill are buried), is carpeted with snowdrops, aconites, blue anemones, violets and primroses and it attracts sightseers from miles around. On a balmy summer evening at evensong, with the bleating of sheep and lambs from the nearby meadows one really feels at peace with the world.

The village has no buildings of great architectural merit and has no great claim to fame. The Underhill Trust, set up in the year 1780 with the sum of £100 by Mrs Margaret Underhill, for the 'benefit and succour of the needy of the Parish' from time to time provides Christmas treats for the elderly. It is the people who make Loxley special and who will continue to do so.

🍁 LUDDINGTON

Luddington is a very pleasant hamlet just three miles from Stratford-upon-Avon, on the river Avon, with beautiful views of the Cotswolds. Some of the cottages are quite old black and white ones, but many have been built since the 1930s.

It is reputed that William Shakespeare married Ann Hathaway in the old chapel which was burnt down towards the end of the 18th century. A new church was consecrated in 1872, built on land given by the Marquis of Hertford – a major landowner – as his contribution towards the new building. All records in the old church were destroyed with the exception of the Bishops Bible dating from 1592 and the old stone font, which have been carefully preserved.

At the Binton end of the lane there was a large notice stating that the road was unsuitable for heavy traffic. Nothing much has been done since then to the road, except that the bridge over the brook has been strengthened and the hump over the discontinued railway has been flattened. In the 1930s there was neither water or sewerage, everyone relied on wells which were not adequate in dry summers and often went brackish. One lady who was expecting a baby wrote to the *Daily Mirror* about her plight and later water pipes were put in by the Italian prisoners of war and standpipes erected. After the war the houses were connected to the water mains. About 1967, the sewer was put in and that did away with cesspits, which were a nuisance because they sometimes overflowed.

Nearly 30 years ago the Avon Trust deepened the river to make it navigable for pleasure boats, and a lock was built and there are now moorings. Unfortunately this has made a vast difference to the wild life on the river, but against this we do not get floods like we used to do. They come up quickly but they are down again in a couple of days.

Luddington is a very friendly place and is fortunate to have a very nice village hall, built in 1957 on land given by Mr C. H. Whitehead. There is no shop or pub. The shop closed in 1988.

Every new resident who comes to live in Luddington is given a letter of welcome and told about the activities of the village – when the dustman calls, the mobile library, the church, the WI and anything else of interest. At the beginning of the 1970s it was thought that the church would have to close, but owing to some excellent parish priests and the welcome letter, we have increased the attendance dramatically. There is also a social side that is very well attended, and a Family Service once a month that the children enjoy very much.

We did not have electricity until 1950 but as we have overhead cables we have to be prepared for cuts in the supply, as snow, heavy frost, winds or thunderstorms can bring the cables down and we have been cut off in the depths of winter for more than 86 hours.

In the 1950s the Luddington Experimental Horticultural Station arrived which absorbed some of the local labour. During the war Sir George Stapleton had been engaged in experimenting in grasslands; later this work was transferred to Aberystwyth.

In the late 1960s the village was on television and in the papers regarding the argument over the ownership of the village green. This was later settled by the village having to pay a token rental to the Marquis of Hertford.

There is a right of way along the river bank and it is possible to walk to Stratford. On the whole Luddington is a quiet village but the traffic has increased dramatically in the last year or two, especially on race days.

In the evenings, just as the sun is going down, a beautiful light comes over the land. It just lasts about five minutes and is a delight to stand and watch.

MANCETTER

Mancetter is situated on a rocky outcrop overlooking the valley of the river Anker. The name Mancetter comes from the Roman Manduessedum. This was a Roman camp on the slight rise on which the church now stands. It was one of a line of forts built as the Romans advanced northwards, the A5 (Watling Street) marking the frontier.

William the Conqueror granted the Manor of Mancetter to his nephew the Earl of Chester, who bestowed it on a Norman knight. He assumed the name of Mancestre and built the church and manor house.

Mancetter Manor was a 14th century house of massive oak framing. Extensions and additions to the front now make it look like a half-timbered gabled house of the Tudor period. Here lived the Mancetter Martyr, Robert Glover and his brothers John and

William. They were active Protestants at a time when Mary Tudor was trying to impose Catholicism on England. Robert, ill in bed at the time, was arrested and was burnt at the stake in Coventry in 1555. John and William escaped, but died of starvation.

A neighbour, Mrs Lewis, also a Protestant, was hidden in a little room off the main bedroom in Manor Farm, but she was eventually burnt at the stake in Lichfield in 1557. There are secret panels in the Manor and a secret passage from Mancetter to Merevale. In the late 1900s the Manor became a hotel and restaurant, but it has now closed and is a private home.

Between the Manor and the church are a row of almshouses, which along with another row opposite the church, were built in 1728 and endowed from the money, £2,000, left by James Gramer, a London goldsmith of Atherstone descent.

Guy de Mancestre started building the first part of the church tower in the 14th century but he died in 1365 before it was finally completed in the 15th century. The north aisle of the church was the chapel of the Bracebridges of Atherstone. The south aisle was the chantry of the convent of Merevale. The east window contains fine stained glass and is thought to have been part of the great Jesse window from Merevale Abbey. Part of this window was made by John Thornton, builder of the great east window of York Minster. The bells in the tower and the east window have recently been restored.

As trade developed in Norman times so the town of Atherstone gradually grew in size and the importance of the village of Mancetter slowly diminished, although the church of Mancetter still remained the mother church.

The Dame school was in a cottage where scholars were charged twopence per week. The next school was built in 1875 with one room only and additions were made as the number of children increased. Unfortunately the village school closed in the 1990s and it is now a private house. The church and the Memorial Hall are the present centres of activity.

There are only two pubs in the village. The 14th century Plough Inn was next to the church and one of the cottages adjacent to it was thought to be the Guild House set up by the

Abbot of Merevale. The Blue Boar Inn was a small place near the smithy and the old Arbor cottages.

The old mill, now in ruins, was down by the river Anker just below the church. The local scouts have built a new headquarters in this lane and the prefabricated council houses in the village have been demolished and replaced with brick ones.

The lovely countryside around Mancetter was part of the Arden Forest and by 1779 there were five mixed farms in the area. Many of the fields around the village are now housing estates with a large recreational ground, although part of the Outwoods is now a golf course and there is limited access to the bluebell woods and the reservoir.

The retaining dam of the reservoir was lined with stone from the Mancetter quarry, which was started in the 19th century. Two quarries merged in 1951, but part of this industry has now closed, as has the last hatting factory in Atherstone (1999) and there are no longer any mining pits in the area.

The canal was used to transport coal and quarry stone, but today is only used for leisure activities. The A5 takes traffic across the river Anker and along the bypass, skirting Mancetter and Atherstone. Local people now work in light industries on the three industrial sites within a two-mile radius of the village, but many also travel to larger towns nearby such as Tamworth, Nuneaton, Hinckley, Coventry and Birmingham.

🍁 MARTON

Marton stands at the confluence of the rivers Leam and Itchin and is dissected by the A423, Coventry to Oxford road. An interesting feature here is the 'Middleton Bridge' over the river Leam, named after John Middleton who was born in the village but became a wealthy mercer in the City of London at the time of Sir Richard (Dick) Whittington. It was built in 1414, possibly to celebrate his retirement as Warden of the Ancient Mercers' Company, and by his intervention the villagers were released from the payment of toll. It is unusual in that it follows the curve of the road and although widened and improved to accommodate modern traffic some of the original stone arches can still be seen. The bridge has become inadequate for the modern lorries and a rebuilding scheme will straighten much of the bend. It will also expose more of the ancient bridge, which will become a footbridge. Within the village a private road to Hockley House Farm crosses the river Itchin via a bridge built by Samuel Shepherd around 1850.

The parish church is dedicated to the Holy Spirit, itself uncommon, but unique here in that the French form, St Esprit, is used. This arises from the granting of the church in the 12th century by King Stephen as a chapel of ease to a French order of nuns originating in Fontvrallt, later installed in Nuneaton. When nearby land was being excavated for building some years ago, several ancient bones were exhumed which experts at Warwick County Museum thought were those of some of the nuns, the dating and location coinciding with the time during which the chapel of ease existed here. This may have a connection with curious rumours of ghostly nuns being seen in Marton, at least one sighting being quite authentic, even though inexplicable. The church was destroyed, possibly by fire, in the 1860s and rebuilt in 1871, although some of the original ancient structure remains.

The village boasts its own Museum of County Bygones, run by a local historian, George Tims, where many artefacts from days gone by, agricultural and domestic, can be seen, all beautifully displayed in a specially constructed building.

Two local butterfly and moth enthusiasts were able during the 1970s to advise the Warwickshire Biological Records Centre of the first recorded Warwickshire sighting of the Varied Coronet (*Hadena Compta*), a Dewicks Plusia (*Mcdunnoughia Confusa*) and a Silver Striped Hawk Moth (*Hippotion Celerio*), the latter the only Warwickshire sighting that century. There is also a colony of Marbled White butterflies, not scarce but rarely seen because they live in very local colonies. Also in the area of natural history, there is still an ancient ridge and furrow field to be seen in the village.

Many interesting and talented people have contributed to the life of the village over the years, and notable among them were

Noel and Barbara Newsome, both talented artists who had exhibited at the Royal Academy. Noel had had a fascinating career, including service with the Ministry of Information during the war and during his time here he worked tirelessly for the village, its church and for conservation. Barbara became the first woman churchwarden at Marton church and her talent as a sculptor was displayed whenever sufficient frozen snow enabled her to do exquisite snow sculptures round the village, which brought traffic chaos when people from miles around came to view them. She also produced large numbers of sunfaces, moulded in cement, and almost every garden in the village boasts one of these. New village signs bought to mark the millennium incorporate the sun-face logo in their design.

Another famous inhabitant of Marton in the past was a racehorse foal named Santa Claus, bred by the local doctor, Frank Smorfitt, which went on to win the Derby in 1964. After feeding him with apples and crusts of bread and watching him career round the paddock after his dam, the villagers cheered him to a man on that June day.

🍁 MAXSTOKE

In the Domesday Book the village was called 'Machitone'. In 1170 according to Pipe Rolls it was 'Makestoke'. This part of Warwickshire was forest and would account for the meaning of a place ending with 'stoke', meaning stockade. Stockades were built as fences for animals for safety from intruders and wolves. 'Max' was from a local man known as 'Macca'.

Sir William de Clinton who built the castle – now lived in by Michael and Rosemary Featherston Dilke and family – founded a 'chantry' on the site of the church in 1333, and dedicated it to St Michael and All Angels. A chantry was an endowed chapel where masses for the dead were sung. In 1342 he developed it into a priory, which played a vital part in the local economy. It kept beef and dairy herds and its produce was sold at Coleshill Market.

The village is much as it was, except that the school has closed.

The golf club is now where the prisoner of war camp was built in the Second World War, overflowing into the park, a much loved place for walks. The village still has its characters – Charlie the mole catcher, with his dry sense of humour, can do any job you want him to and will always have a tale to tell. He will always be particularly remembered for his work of relaying the path of the church – a real work of art.

The farms are now edged with a motorway and criss-crossed with gas and fuel pipelines, and underneath all that is a coal mine, but still the farmers carry on.

🍁 MIDDLETON

This village is like an island, situated in a network of motorways. Hamlets, e.g. Hunts Green, Allen End, Hill Lane, cover a radius of 15 miles and make up the village. Middleton is five miles from Tamworth and five miles from Sutton Coldfield, and the name probably indicated the midway position between these two towns.

Both the church and the village are recorded in the Conqueror's Domesday Book. The village school which was built in 1886 was originally a Church School, and had as many as 100 pupils at one time. It was finally closed in July 1994. Fortunately for the village the Parish Council was able to purchase the school building from the Educational Authority to become a community centre for the residents of Middleton.

The church is St John the Baptist and goes back to Anglo-Saxon times. No trace of the Saxon church remains, for the church was rebuilt in the Norman style, probably towards the end of the 12th century. The church which has a tower, once had a steeple. The nave is divided from the chancel by a fine medieval screen. On the north wall of the chancel is the 'Lepers Squint'. There is a sculpture of two half brothers, Benjamin and Samuel White, whose father, Samuel White, was one of the principal benefactors of Middleton. The story is that one day he passed through the village and saw some hungry looking children. He was so moved by this that he decided to give money for the poor of the parish. As a result of his benefactions, six almshouses have been built (1966) and doles were distributed to the widows, the old and the needy, and at Whitsuntide every child received a Whit loaf. The original base of the cross still remains in the churchyard.

The Lady Middleton Charity and Middleton United Foundation are two charities for the young and the old of the village. Lady Middleton left money for a bible to be given to every school leaver. Middleton United Foundation gives help for educational expenses of the young students of the village.

For many generations the Willoughby family occupied Middleton Hall. The Hall had two Royal visitors. Queen Elizabeth I, who it is said called on her way to Coventry and gave Sir Hugh Willoughby his Knighthood, and James I, who stayed there on his journey from Scotland and knighted Sir Percival Willoughby who had then inherited the Hall. Hugh Willoughby was an explorer. The Hall was a moated residence, but in the year 1868 the occupier decided to do away with the moat. It is now being restored back to a moated residence. A skeleton of a horse and rider in armour was discovered in the moat and the rider was thought to be a Courier 'Messenger' in the Royalist Army when the battle of Edgehill in Warwickshire was fought on 23rd October 1642 and that the rider was leaving the hall one night in a dense fog when he lost his bearings and instead of making for the bridge, crossed the quadrangle and tripped over the parapet into the moat. The human bones were buried in the churchyard and the gauntlet glove and helmet are displayed in the chancel of Middleton church. Mr John Ray who stayed in Middleton Hall in 1666 as a tutor, was a naturalist. Ray's plant records from the Middleton neighbourhood contribute almost 40 of the first species recorded for Warwickshire plus some first species recordings for the British Isles dating from his works at Middleton.

In 1966, the last tenants of the Hall were the Averill family and they moved out due to the state of gradual deterioration. In 1978, Mr Peter Thomas of The Vicarage, Middleton, formed a trust known as Middleton Hall Trust. This Trust has gone from strength to strength and now has a large membership. The building is being repaired and improved. Many evening and weekend events take place. Bird hides have been erected and the wall garden restored.

The village stocks were located next to the Green Man public house. This building was once a farmhouse and a family named Stevenson were publicans for 100 years. There was a club room in the public house, which was used for the rents to be paid.

Most villages have their ghosts and Middleton is no exception. Residents talk of a figure dressed in black silk walking from the church to a nearby cottage every Hallowe'en!

🍁 MORETON MORRELL

In olden times the manor consisted of the town of Moreton and the hamlet of Morrell, and 40 years ago another residential development was added at Moreton Paddox. Entering Moreton from the north one passes a recent development of 36 houses, bordering John Taylor Way, before passing Fuller Place, and Oak Tree Close – a 1960s sympathetic development of 44 houses round a central green. Mr Fuller built the shop/post office in 1910, and was active in every aspect of village life, including long service as a district councillor, while John Taylor planted and tended roadside trees to replace the elms lost through disease circa 1974.

Further on, to the left a road leads out of Duffus Hill into Middletown and the cottage where William Randolph was born in 1651. Emigrating to Virginia in 1672, he was the ancestor of Thomas Jefferson, third President of the USA. In the treed area at the corner with Brook Lane there was once a dove house, hence the name Duffus Hill.

Proceeding along the Street, the 17th century Moreton House was built on the site of a chantry house belonging to the Hospital of St John, Warwick. Next to the friendly Black Horse pub is the black and white, thatched 16th century Well Cottage, and beyond the village hall – the 19th century village school – is another similar cottage.

Opposite the latter is the popular and successful Moreton

Morrell C of E primary school. Built as two classrooms in 1914, permanent extensions in the last 50 years include hall, indoor cloakrooms, offices, kitchen and two classrooms. Having over 110 pupils, an extra classroom is to be built shortly.

Beyond the shop is the church of the Holy Cross adjacent to the 16th century Manor House. A priest was mentioned in the Domesday Book, and the oldest part of the church is the 12th century base of the tower. Above the churchyard is the Wellingtonia-lined drive leading to the Moreton Morrell Centre of Warwickshire College, originally the Farm Institute established at Moreton Hall in 1949.

A hundred years ago this was largely an agricultural community served by local tradesmen such as the baker, blacksmith, butcher and carpenter. Only the pub and the shop survive, whilst commuters double the population.

🍁 NAPTON-ON-THE-HILL

For centuries two buildings have dominated the skyline of Napton village; high above the houses rise the outlines of the ancient church and the impressive windmill. The angular sails are silhouetted against a background of seasonal skies; they are dramatic against the greyness of winter or stark before the cloud-scudding cobalt of summer. Seven counties are said to be visible from the top of this 500 foot hill on a fine day and it is probable that an Iron Age fort once crowned its summit.

The name Napton means 'village on the hilltop', from the Anglo-Saxon 'cnaepp' meaning hilltop and 'tun' meaning settlement. It is recorded as Neptone in the Domesday Book. By the Middle Ages it had become one of the largest towns in Warwickshire. Unusually, the population was almost the same as today with approximately 1,000 people living within its boundaries. It possessed at least three manors and a charter was granted by Edward II in the 14th century giving it the right to hold a weekly Thursday market and an annual three day fair to be held 'even-day and morrow after the Feast of the Assumption of the Blessed Virgin' (August 14, 15 and 16th). Neither market nor fair exist any longer.

In many places in and around Npaton, may be seen extensive medieval strip systems where long departed villagers grew their crops and it remains basically an agricultural community. Unlike much of Warwickshire, Napton was not part of the vast Forest of Arden, but was 'feldon' or agricultural land which was not densely wooded. Local houses were stone built and not timbered as in neighbouring areas.

The De Napton family lived in one of the long lost manors until their last heir, a girl named Jana married Adam, one of the Shuckburgh family during the 14th century. Since that time Napton and Shuckburgh, two miles distant have been linked in many ways and are now part of the same parish group together with neighbouring Stockton.

The church of St Lawrence dates from the 12th century, was rebuilt in the 13th century and has later additions. Originally the rector of Napton was the Prior of Coventry who received its tithes but engaged a vicar to perform his parochial duties. Marks on either side of the chancel arch seem to indicate that the building once possessed a rood screen. Until quite recently a large gallery stretched across the west end of the building and is remembered by older parishioners. On the vestry door is a strange grille covered by a heavy shutter. Nobody knows the purpose for which it was intended: a spy hole or maybe a confessional; who can tell? An ancient wooden chest dated 1624 and given by Thomas and Isabel Garret of Napton is one of the church's treasures: rustic in style but a tangible link with past worshippers in this holy place.

In common with other hilltop villages, there is a legend which tells how the original church was to have been built near to the present village green. Each night however, the stones which lay ready for construction were transported by 'fairies' or 'spirits' to the summit of Napton hill. The villagers took the hint and the church duly arose on the hill-top overlooking the village nestling below, and its squat tower has withstood the buffeting winds for centuries.

The church has six bells and these are regularly rung by a

team of enthusiastic bell-ringers who occasionally enjoy the challenge of a Quarter Peal. An old set of hand bells still exist and their sweet notes still ring out joyfully at Christmas and other festivals. Napton possesses its very own Christmas carol entitled *Fleecy Care*. This was probably written by a local person in the late 18th or early 19th century, and it was bellowed out by local men during the festive season, often after their tonsils had been well oiled with ale.

Two grey gowned Elizabethan ladies are said to haunt the church. They kneel in the front pew quietly praying. During the early 19th century a visiting clergyman, the Reverend Augustus Fent, returned late one evening to collect a forgotten cassock and in the dim light was surprised to see two ladies there so late, but he wished them good-night and passed on. Next day he was told that the ghostly 'parishioners' were regular worshippers. Several present day villagers say they have seen them but who they are nobody knows.

The old Methodist chapel was, until recently, a Nickelodeon theatre and is now being converted into a house. The Christadelphian chapel on Pillory Green is still in use and the Congregational chapel is a private house.

Chapel Green, on the edge of the village is named after a 14th century chapel which once stood on the site. Nothing of it now remains but excavations have revealed Roman and Saxon relics and it is probable that an earlier village was situated here. Nearby is the old Welsh Road, along which drovers walked their cattle from the distant Welsh hills to the markets of Buckingham and London.

The most dramatic building in Napton is undoubtedly the windmill, which was restored in recent years. Originally there were two mills and old maps clearly show them situated quite close together. Records of the mill date back to 1543 but it is probable that an earlier mill existed on the site. A spring and well lie within the grounds going deep down into the hillside and providing a never failing supply of pure water.

There is a footpath leading down from the windmill to what used to be the Napton Brick and Tile works where a large

Napton Locks

proportion of villagers used to earn their livings. Bricks and tiles marked with the windmill stamp were produced from local clay and fired in the longest kiln in Europe. They were transported by canal boats which moored alongside the works on the Oxford canal. A small industrial site now occupies the site.

The Oxford canal, constructed in the 18th century, sweeps around Napton on three sides and is a contour canal and not a 'cut', as it follows the lowest natural features of the countryside, creating a pleasant meandering route unlike most other waterways. During the 1950s the canal was in danger of being abandoned, but the coming of pleasure craft saved its life, and now colourful narrow boats ply its length and three marinas bring pleasure and employment to the area. The Grand Union and Oxford canals join up at Napton and the old wide basins provided for converging boats remain. Old boatmen, often transporting Napton bricks, used Napton windmill as a landmark.

Local family names such as Sheasby, Eadon, Duckett and Griffin still exist amongst the villagers. Napton was famous for the nicknames it gave its residents and appellations such as Squelch Duckett, Wag Green, Snodger Cox, Waggo Alsop, Grunt Griffin, Fligger Tarrant, Shirty Balsam, Traddles Eadon and Faggy Duckett are recorded.

Until 1948 Napton had separate schools for boys and girls but at that time they amalgamated and became St Lawrence Church of England School for mixed infants and juniors. Local secondary schools received the older pupils on them reaching twelve years of age. Now that school too has closed and the children transferred to a large new building which was opened in 1997 to serve the needs of Napton and surrounding villages. Education has come a long way since children were taught on the stone benches of the church porch.

Napton remains a lively and attractive place in which to live with an active community who enjoy the various clubs and sporting activities as well as rural pleasures. The Windmill Singers are a local musical group who entertain people all over the county and every year a village pantomime is produced which creates hilarious entertainment for the villagers' enjoyment.

An old gentleman of over 80 who had lived in the village all his life, was taken to visit the seaside for the very first time. On returning home he was asked his opinion of the mighty ocean and after pausing he replied, 'It's no better than Napton ressy' (ressy – a local name for the reservoir). Like that old man, many people living in Napton feel that it is a beautiful and impressive place in which to live, and one which bears comparison with other lovely Warwickshire villages.

The folk who live on the hill welcome you to their village.

🍁 NEWBOLD-ON-AVON

In step with other villages, people and places in Newbold have changed dramatically over the years. Main Street now boasts a Balti restaurant and a fish and chip shop, a beauty salon, a television and video repair shop, and a car salesroom, as well as the mini-supermarket and post office, and the butcher's shop which has recently changed hands. The Clark brothers retired and their mother, at over 100 years old, decided to stop working in the shop.

The village hall (the old school, built in the mid 1800s) is flourishing and well used, and the two schools are expanding to include a nursery class in one and ages 11 and 12 in the other.

Newbold Rugger Club has a certain standing in the Midlands, especially with the tradition and proximity of Rugby School where it all started.

St Botolph's church stands just below the summit of a hill, overlooking the village. It was built in the 15th century on the site of an earlier church. To the right of the chancel arch can be seen part of the early 14th century tiled floor of the previous church. An incised slab under the arch in the south wall is to Thomas and Elizabeth Boughton and is dated 1454. It may be that this arch tomb indicates that they were responsible for the rebuilding of the church at that time. The organ is dated about 1800 and is believed to have come from Rugby School chapel in 1858. The tower contains eight bells. The clock, dated 1795, is by Sam Dalton of Rugby, and the weathervane, designed in 1975, represents St Botolph, the original patron saint of travellers, with his pack-donkey.

Diagonally across the churchyard can be seen the sunken line of an old arm of the Oxford Canal which served brickworks and quarries between Newbold and Rugby. This was closed in 1840, but one end of the tunnel can be seen from the field behind the tower. The Oxford Canal flows past the village through one of the longest tunnels in the area – roughly a quarter of a mile. Years ago the canal was used to carry coal, by horse and barge, all over the Midlands. Now it is used for leisure with motorised barges and boats. This brings a lot of visitors to the village and increased business to the local shops.

At one time the top half of the village was closed off by a gate across the road and now on one corner is one of the three public houses, which have all been improved and enlarged. Several small enclaves of new housing have been built, and a bridge, opened by the then Mayor in December 1971, has alleviated flooding problems and helps to unite the two parts of the village.

The skyline is now dominated by the massive works at Rugby Cement, visible from all parts of the village. The old quarry has now become Newbold Quarry Park, and extensive works have made it a beauty spot, well used by anglers, strollers and dog-walkers.

❧ NEWBOLD-ON-STOUR

The village of Newbold-on-Stour probably started as a cluster of cottages around a toll house and inn (both still standing), six miles south of Stratford-upon-Avon on the road to Shipston-on-Stour and Oxford. It is still not much more. Most buildings are Georgian or Victorian or later.

An exception is Ettington Park which, despite its name, is at the northern end of Newbold. The Victorian house, recently restored after a fire, is an hotel, but it and the park are owned by the Shirley family, who are believed to be the only family left who can claim to still own the land they held at the Norman Conquest.

Also on Shirley land alongside the river Stour is the headquarters of Newbold-on-Stour Sea Scout Troop, which is the sea scout troop furthest from the sea. Founded in 1957 and still thriving, the troop is one of the select band of 100 holding Royal Navy recognition.

The village made local news in 1912 with a devastating fire. A row of cottages with thatched roofs opposite the Victorian parish church caught fire and sparks travelled about 100 yards to another row of thatched cottages and they were all destroyed. A horse-drawn manual fire engine was taken down a track to the river and hoses led to the fire, but without effect. Those cob-walled cottages have been replaced with brick-walled, slate-roofed houses, now mainly occupied by commuters.

The only thatched building left in the village is known as the bothy, probably 300 years old. It has thick cob walls and has recently been rethatched. It stands on the village green near the village hall, which was built to replace a wooden hut in the 1950s. The dividing line between the common and Shirley land passes through the foundations. As the Shirleys did not wish to part with any of their long-held land, rights had to be negotiated.

The river Stour provided power for a large number of mills. All are now gone or converted into residences, but the last to go was Talton Mill, where the Holberton family now farm and sell produce.

A notable village craftsman was the saddler Mr J. Rimell, with a reputation that brought in work from a wide area. He had a regular standby contract to make large numbers of martingales to take horse brasses made in Birmingham and sold in America. He died in 1975, but a village road is named after him and his apprentice continues the trade under his name in Shipston-on-Stour.

At Armscote on the south side of the village there is a Quaker Meeting House. It attracts Quakers from all over the country on the first Sunday in August each year, as it was one of the last stopping places of George Fox, when he was being hounded across the country.

About 1910 Primitive Methodists held meetings in the kitchen of the end cottage of the row later burned down. It is said the preacher sat on the copper and the congregation sat on forms. They built the Methodist church, which is hard against the busy A3400 road. The church has recently been renovated, and services are held there every Sunday.

The Victorian parish church, St David's, is also used regularly. The present priest-in-charge lives in neighbouring Tredington, while the old Newbold Rectory is known as The Grange and is a private house.

In 1999, after some opposition from villagers, a large housing estate of 50 houses was built on the southern outskirts of Newbold, which has increased the population of the village by about fifty per cent. The Church school, which had been threatened with closure many times, has been amalgamated with Tredington School as one school on two sites. Newbold houses the younger children and has a flourishing nursery. The new housing estate has at least ensured the demand for a school in the village. There is also a flourishing village shop and post office, two pubs and a bowling green.

❧ NEWBOLD PACEY & ASHORNE

Newbold Pacey is the older of the two places, Newbold Pacey being at one time the village and Ashorne the hamlet. Local folklore says that Ashorne came about when a gentleman named Edward Carew came to Newbold Pacey to escape the plague in London, but brought it with him. The villagers then crossed Oozley Brook to escape the plague and built their houses in Ashorne. Ashorne is an Anglo-Saxon word for north-east, so it signifies the north-east corner of the parish.

There is a monument to Edward Carew and his infant daughter in the church. This monument was brought from the previous church which was partly wooden. The present church was designed by J. L. Pearson, who was also the architect of Truro cathedral. There are a few interesting monuments in the church, one to a past vicar who was nephew of the poet Southey and another to somebody who was,

'a martyr to the gout.'

It is rumoured that a lot of the cottages in Newbold Pacey were burnt down and never rebuilt so that only a few remain today. The old vicarage has an exact replica in Virginia, USA. In Ashorne the oldest houses are around the Green, except Stonehouse Farm House, which is mentioned in the Domesday Book. Several of the houses are wattle and daub, the marl being collected from the 'Holloway', which is now a 'C' class road. At one time this was the only way in and out of the village.

In more recent times the village has built a new village hall, which replaced a hut dating from the First World War. Unfortunately, the village has lost its school, post office and shop. The chapel has been sold and converted into a house.

One of the local large houses, Ashorne Hill, was once owned by Mr Bryant of Bryant and May Matches, and was bought by the iron and steel industry during the Second World War as their headquarters. It is now a management college.

There is a cricket field which is the only one in the country where you cross water to get from the pavilion to the field. In the adjoining Ashorne House, at one time, lived Major Bouch, whose uncle was the builder of the doomed Tay Bridge.

As in countless English villages, Newbold and Ashorne now have little to offer in the way of employment. Thus, families which have lived in the parish for many generations must look elsewhere for jobs. As they commute to nearby towns, so do the newcomers to the village. There are still a significant number of family names which also appeared in the 1851 census, and whose grandparents feature, as children, in the 1869–70 Log Book of the village school.

🍁 NEWTON REGIS

This is the northernmost parish in Warwickshire, the name of which probably derives from its former royal ownership under Henry II (reigned 1154–1189). It has also been known as Kings Newton, and, more picturesquely, as Newton-in-the-Thistles (from early in the 18th century). It is not known whether these were abundant wild thistles or specially-grown teasles, used in the carding of flax fibre for linen production. Flax was grown in Newton and linen looms worked in the house now The Queens Head inn.

The village boasts another royal connection. King Charles I prayed at the church before going into battle during the Civil War.

The cathedral in Birmingham was indirectly named after a Newton Regis family. The Phillips family of Newton Hall owned property in Birmingham, and it was Robert Phillips who gave the site of the church, as well as contributing towards its building, 1711–1725. St Philip's church became the cathedral in 1905. The Phillips family married into the Inge family of Thorpe Constantine, just over the border in Staffordshire.

The church, which contains much of historical interest, was originally a chapel to the church at Seckington. The present building is basically 14th century. A singular feature of the village is 'the rock', an outcrop of stone worn into terraces, alongside the pavement opposite the church. The picturesque duck pond in the middle of the village is a quarry pit into which a stream was diverted. A variety of ducks now benefit from this former water supply to the village. They have had a special sign erected by the Council to warn motorists of the habit of the ducks of processing across the road to the farmyard where they live.

A recently instituted annual event happens on New Year's Day, when many villagers turn out with their pets for a three-mile 'Goose Walk', named because one of the founders of the walk used to take his goose with him. Now it is mostly dogs and people.

The village has a popular pub, The Queens Head, a village hall and a bowling green. This is one of the least spoilt villages in

North Warwickshire, whose imposing farmhouses and half timbered thatched cottages have not been obscured by recent small developments.

🍁 No Man's Heath

No Man's Heath is a small village on the B5493 with a short but interesting history. Before the 19th century No Man's Heath was heathland which belonged to neither of the adjoining parishes. A community of 'squatters' developed and the church was built in 1863. By 1871 the population was 122. Some residents still remember the 'mud hut', a thatched one-storey cottage that stood where the Community Centre now is. The church is now closed. The main road from Tamworth to Ashby lost its status as an A route following the opening of the M42. The village has a petrol station on the main road and two garages for vehicle repairs.

One of the first residents of No Man's Heath was Joe Leavesley, a leper. He worked as a coal heaver, and a former Newton Regis resident, Thomas Riley (born 1847), who remembered him described him thus: 'How I looked with dread at the poor man's arm inflamed and scaly as with sleeve turned up he went about his work as a coal heaver with his horse and cart'. He goes on: 'He was the first I believe to build a hut on No Man's Heath, on the Heath itself, not on the fringe of it, in defiance of a neighbouring squire.'

The public house, The Four Counties, records the fact that No Man's Heath used to be the meeting point for the four counties of Warwickshire, Staffordshire, Leicestershire and Derbyshire. The border of Derbyshire has now moved a few miles away, but this heathland became a convenient escape route for fugitives from the law to cross over into a neighbouring county and so evade capture. It was also the site of many prize fights in the 19th century, perhaps for the same reason.

🍁 NORTON LINDSEY

The south Warwickshire village of Norton Lindsey is surrounded by open countryside, and lies four miles away from the county town of Warwick, and six from Stratford-upon-Avon. The adult population, according to the electoral roll, numbers just over 300, and they were proud to have won the accolade of Best Kept Village in the county in 1999.

The nucleus of the village is around the main street and the road leading to the church. The majority of the older houses are in this area. Their names bear witness to the former nature of the village: Barn Cottage, the Old Barn, Stable Cottage, the Old Forge, and so forth. Most of the former farmhouses, such as the White House, have shed their land, and only one working farm, Cannings, remains in the centre of the village, though there are others on the periphery.

Holy Trinity church, which dates back to the 13th century and has an 11th century font, stands in an oasis of peace and quiet, surrounded by the churchyard and the garden of rest. Since 1925, the parish has formed part of the United Benefice of Norton Lindsey, Wolverton and Langley, with the rector living in Wolverton.

The village school, Wolverton Primary, was built in 1876 near the boundary of the two parishes to provide for the children of Norton Lindsey and Wolverton. The school successfully fought off attempts to close it and now flourishes with over 70 pupils. Its academic standards are among the highest in the county.

The western gales account for the village's nickname of 'Windy Lindsey', and they will have done their share in turning the sails of the village windmill, which was built between 1793 and 1800, falling into disuse, it is thought, in 1906. It was here that an unfortunate miller, William Blakeman, died as a result of a fall while setting the sail cloths, on 14th March 1892. Now the mill forms an interesting feature in the garden of the Mill House.

The village hall is used for a myriad of social activities, including the Youth Club, WI, and the Bridge Club, not to mention the many parties, dances and dinners. Smaller social functions take place in the recently refurbished Church Room, which was originally a Victorian dame school. Another popular meeting place in the centre of the village is the local hostelry, The New Inn. Sporting interests are well catered for by the flourishing football and cricket clubs. Although the village no longer has a shop or post office, it is still a thriving and vibrant community!

❦ OLD MILVERTON

It may well be that 'all roads lead to Rome', but only two roads lead to Old Milverton – Old Milverton Lane (a right turn when travelling from Kenilworth to Leamington Spa), and Old Milverton Road (a left turn when approaching Leamington Spa from Warwick), and where these two roads converge there is Old Milverton village.

St James' church marks the end of the route for cars but there are pleasant walks across the fields to the Saxon mill at Guy's Cliffe or into Leamington Spa via Rock Mill Lane. It is said that there is an underground passage from the church to Manor Farm, where, until 1940, there was a 9-hole golf course. The church cemetery contains the graves of the parents of Shirley Williams, the politician, Sir George Catlin and Vera Brittain, the author of *Testament of Youth* and campaigner for feminist rights. Dr Henry Jephson is also buried there. He was a local doctor and regarded almost as the 'patron saint' of Leamington Spa. He helped to establish the high reputation and fame of the town as a spa and its loveliest gardens are named after him.

The fields – Cottage Close, Church Paddocks, Bull Field by the river Avon, Mossy Meadow, and the Pound where stray animals would be held (it lies near to today's bus shelter) – surround only a few houses. There is no inn or shop, and never has been in living memory, although at one time there was a post office in the front room of a cottage.

The village is part of the Heber Percy estate and members of the family had the Parish Room, or village hall, built for use as a

The Parish Church of St James, Old Milverton

Sunday School. Opposite the hall is an ancient barn, which retains an old warning 'Man traps and spring guns on these premises.'

Lady Percy used to present Old Milverton girls with red cloaks and the boys with blue jerseys to keep them warm on the long walk into Leamington Spa to go to school.

The big day in the village is the Horticultural Show and Fete, usually held on the first Saturday in September, when the normally quiet, narrow lane is filled with the cars of visitors and exhibitors.

OVER WHITACRE

Over Whitacre is set in the gently rolling hills of north Warwickshire, halfway from everywhere to anywhere: Birmingham to the west, Tamworth to the north, and

139

Atherstone, Nuneaton and Coventry to the east and south. Sadly it can no longer be described as a quiet country parish as it is now quartered by busy roads. There have been many changes in the last decade. The population has considerably increased to 374, but the inhabitants are now urban workers not farm labourers. The village shop and post office have closed. One of the few

Over Whitacre Church

remaining collieries in the Midlands lies within the parish. However the modern, privately owned Daw Mill Colliery is fortunately tucked into a valley so that only the lights at night are visible.

In the valley by the Bourne river, the settlement of Furnace End grew up around a water mill used for iron smelting. The wealthy and influential North Warwickshire Jennens family established this iron forge in the second half of the 17th century. Charles Jennens became well known as Handel's patron, commissioning him to design the now famous organ in Packington church. He also wrote the libretto for *The Messiah*. The water mill had been left untouched until recently when, with adjoining farm buildings, it was transformed into an award winning residential development.

At the top of the hill, with a view for miles, is St Leonard's church, built in 1766 by a squire who wanted something fashionable. He replaced a medieval church with this Georgian gem – one of the few small churches built in this style of the period in Warwickshire.

With the changes in farming practice, much of the meadowland around the village is now ploughed up to produce maize and potatoes. In spite of all the changes, this parish, with its gentle rolling hills, bluebell woods, natural ponds and the river attracts many ramblers using our network of public footpaths.

🍁 OXHILL

Oxhill is a name which suggests oxen on a hill, but in fact it is derived from Ohtan Scylf (roughly meaning Ohta's ledge of land, or hill). In the Domesday Book (where a mill is recorded) it is spelled Octeselve. In 1183 Robert de Stafford granted the monks of Bordesley 12 acres of land 'on the torrent (stream) of Oxhill where my oxherds dwell'. It would appear that the homely connection with oxen was brought about as a result of changes in spelling!

At one end of the main street is the village hall, originally a

Board school, opened in 1876 and closed after the Second World War, since when Oxhill children have travelled to school in neighbouring Tysoe. There is an attractive inn, The Peacock, and further along is the Methodist church, built in 1814 (cottage meetings having been held since 1769) and extended in 1839. Two years later the Sunday School was started, and in 1880 there were celebrations for the centenary of Robert Raikes having founded the first Sunday School (in Gloucester).

At the head of the street is the old church of St Lawrence. There are the remains of a preaching cross near to the north door. The building still retains its original doorways and chancel arch, dating from the mid 12th century. A priest's doorway is probably 14th century, and a 12th century font has curious carvings of Adam and Eve. Not to be missed, at the west end of the church, are six 15th century oak benches, and a fine screen to the tower (originally forming part of a 15th century chancel screen).

In the churchyard, south-east of the church, there is a most interesting little headstone. The inscription is as follows:

'Here lyeth Myrtella, negro body slave to Mr. Thomas Beauchamp, Gent, of Nevis. Bapt. Oct ye 26th and buried ye Jan. 6th 1705'.

Mr Thomas Beauchamp is believed to have been a sugar planter, which would explain this neat headstone, so unexpected in an English village.

🍁 PACKINGTON

All the inhabitants love this part of the Forest of Arden, whether it be Great or Little Packington. The community existed long before the Norman Conquest, many Roman and Stone Age relics having been found. That it was of some prosperity is indicated by the existence of two mills which served a local population of about 60. Its taxation value was 30 shillings, compared with the 20 shillings of its humbler neighbour Birmingham.

The rural church is its focal point. Unfortunately, Little Packington church became redundant, but has now been converted to a family dwelling. However, Great Packington church still proudly looms large in people's lives. In 1278 the de Clintons of Maxstoke gave it to Kenilworth Priory and thus it remained until the Dissolution of the Monasteries, which gave Henry VIII the opportunity to sell it for £626 to the sitting tenant John Fisher, 'who served with King Henry VIII, King Edward VI, Queen Mary and Queen Elizabeth in Court as Gentleman – Pensioner to them all', a remarkable achievement in such troubled times. Subsequent generations of Fishers served as Lords of the Manor until 1712 when the 2nd Earl of Aylesford married Mary Fisher.

The present building is a strange-looking structure set in the middle of Packington Park. Its appearance belies the beauty of the interior, in which the eye is drawn to the altar-piece by Rigaud, depicting the Ascension. The church is listed on two counts as historically and architecturally important, for in 1789 the building that the Fishers knew was demolished to make way for a brand new church by the 4th Earl of Aylesford as a public thanksgiving for the recovery of George III from his mental illness.

The building houses a chamber organ designed by Handel for his patron, Charles Jennens, who bequeathed it to his cousins, the Aylesfords. This forms the centre-piece of the annual concert by the Choral and Organ Scholars of King's College, Cambridge. A curious feature in one of the cupolas is the Great Bell. Originally there was a peal of three, but in 1805 the inhabitants in their zealous excitement to celebrate the victory at Trafalgar brought them crashing to the ground. They were melted down to form one Great Bell with a Latin inscription round its lip recalling the mishap, together with a medallion of George III.

There is no actual village in either parish. Great Packington is indicated by no signpost, while Little Packington infuriates all strangers, who are baffled by the way the river bisects its 1,500 acres across which its 14 houses are scattered. Here at the Ford, formerly called Packington Green, before the 18th century Enclosures, the main road from Meriden having passed through the deer park of Great Packington, crossed on its way to Coleshill and Lichfield.

Now there is only one footpath, and not many realise that the medieval due of one shilling is still handed over by the undertaker to the Earl, to permit the passage of a corpse to the churchyard, thus safeguarding the private ownership of the Park, for the free passage of a dead body formerly created a right of way. Indications of former tenants abound in place names: we find Flint's Wood (he was a Catholic who was fined for refusing to go to the Anglican church), Geary's Heath (there was a parson of that name), Dial's Pool, Mulliner's Rough, Butler's End, Todd's Rough and Keatley's Pool. Even more intriguing is Paddy's Path (along the line of an old footpath beside the 'main road') and Jones's Knob – both on rising ground opposite Rookwood, former home of the novelist George Eliot's brother when he was land agent for the Aylesford's Packington estate.

Seven farms surround the 500 acre park and at the northern end lies a 400 acre landfill site, the largest in Europe, from which sand and gravel were formerly extracted and which is now a conservation award winner. Old sand and gravel workings are transformed into a trout fishery and golf course on the eastern borders, also awarded a conservation prize.

The Packingtons today – in spite of being surrounded by a motorway and major trunk roads – continue to be an unspoiled rural community owned by the 11th Earl of Aylesford. Following a fire at Packington Hall in 1979 the Earl and Countess made the Old Hall their home and since the death of the Countess, the Earl continues to reside there, while their heir, Lord Guernsey, and his family live at the Hall. Both houses stand in the picturesque deer park, home of 400 rare black-backed fallow deer, roaming freely amongst the old woodland and several lakes.

🍁 PAILTON

Pailington it used to be. The records of the village and its families go back to the days when Danes and Saxons lived in close proximity if not in complete amity. It is set in beautiful country, an agricultural area where life is perhaps not so rushed as in a town.

Over the centuries the village lands have been divided into various areas and belonged to various Lords of the Manor. Family names going back many years are still found here. Buswell, Bailey, Harrison, Skipworth and of course, the Earls of Denbigh. These names are all on a map dated 1762 which was based on the Pailton enclosure award. Some land was owned by Trinity College, Cambridge, and it held the leasehold and right to collect tithes for a fixed rent from the tenants.

Its church, dedicated to St Denis, was built in 1884 and had a major overhaul in 1982 because of the presence of dry rot. Pailton Hall, in the centre of the village, was left by Lady Mary Feilding, the twin sister of the Earl of Denbigh, to the Archdeacon of Coventry and the Vicar of Monks Kirby for the benefit of 'respectable' inhabitants of the parish of Monks Kirby. The income, at her death, went towards the salary of the curate of the parish. Eventually five trustees were appointed to administer the income and the property. They were responsible to the Charity Commissioners. The Hall was sold in 1986.

Over the years the village has changed of course. The school was bombed during the Second World War and not rebuilt. Since then the schoolchildren have always travelled by bus to the schools in Monks Kirby. The old village hall became a private house and to replace it the Mission Hall in Lutterworth Road was purchased as the new village hall. A few new houses have been built within the village boundaries, older houses have been modernised and fresh blood has come to the village to make a friendly, caring community.

There is a thriving pub where various village gatherings are held and a village shop which has been in the same hands since 1969. A thriving coach business started from small beginnings by Harry Lewis with a brougham and a dog cart in 1907. He charged 5s.6d to Rugby station and 3s. to Brinklow station. Today his grandson, Norman, has enlarged the business greatly and it is possible to board a luxurious coach in the village and be transported to various parts of Europe and be returned to one's own doorstep.

145

At the centre of the village where three roads meet, from Coventry, Rugby, and Lutterworth, there used to be a village pump and war memorial but, alas, the pump has disappeared. The village used to have its own bakehouse and it was a great pleasure in the early morning to collect hot bread and watch the dough being put into the baking oven with its glowing fire underneath, and when cooked, taken out with the long handled shovel. Modernisation and the big firms took over and all that remains now is the name The Bakehouse.

Pailton Radio Station was established by the RAF in 1940. 1946 saw it taken over by the Ministry of Civil Aviation. Sputnik I, the first earth satellite, was heard there in October 1957. Since 1946 the buildings have been extended considerably and the number of staff employed has increased.

🍁 POLESWORTH

Polesworth is a large village at the tip of north Warwickshire, bordering on Staffordshire and Leicestershire, and to reach it one has to cross a bridge of some kind. There are two railways, three canals and a wide bridge over the river Anker.

From the river bridge, looking eastwards, one can see the beautiful Abbey church and vicarage. The accepted date of the foundation of the Abbey is AD 827. Polesworth got its name from 'Pol' meaning deep water and 'Worth' being a dwelling.

It is a place steeped in history. William Shakespeare and Michael Drayton, the poet, were purported to be visitors to Pooley Hall and the vicarage. Pooley Hall is an ancient manor house with chapel, overlooking the river and meadows. Thomas Cockayne who built the hall in 1507 was slain on his way to church by his feuding neighbour, Thomas Burdet from Bramcote Hall – a true but sorry tale.

Among the ancient buildings remaining is a tithe barn, beautifully restored, and now a very useful amenity for the village. There are a few cottages, a dovecote, the Nethersole Centre which was originally a school, and the Nunnery Gateway, which is the entrance way to the church. Yes, long ago, there were nuns in Polesworth and they taught needlework to the girls of the village. In the 17th century, Sir Francis Nethersole had founded a school so that boys and girls could have a free education.

The lovely thatched house in the Square which was once a landmark, the flour mill by the river and Little Jim's Cottage have long since gone. There is a poem in print about 'Little Jim', the collier's son.

Polesworth was one of the first villages to have electricity, a luxury indeed if only for lighting. It was generated at Pooley Hall colliery. The colliery was acquired by a New Zealand family named Chaytor who had also purchased Pooley Hall with its lands in the late 1800s. In the Lawn Field, near the colliery where there is a monument to the colliers who gave their lives in the First World War, an annual gymkhana used to be held and hundreds of people enjoyed this special day. The pit ponies enjoyed it too because they came up for an airing and a welcome graze.

The canal winds its way through Polesworth and years ago, the local firm of Lees and Atkins built and repaired narrow boats at Polesworth docks. A family member painted them with lovely roses and castles. The winters long ago were very severe, and most people could skate. They would skate by moonlight on the frozen canal and if there was no moon, they lit candles and placed them on either side. Villagers formed their own concert party and Morris dancing troupe and there seemed to be as many pubs as villagers. In fact, there is only one less pub today and the population now is approximately 8,000.

In 1912 a cinema was opened in a converted flour mill. This delighted the villagers who enjoyed the serial films which were included. On Saturday afternoons there was a children's matinee with comedies and westerns. Private apartments have now been built on the site near to the canal where the cinema used to be.

With the closure of the colliery and the clay works, which had chimneys that belched out the most dreadful smoke and sulphur fumes, most workers today have to commute to nearby towns and cities. However, now that the M42 has been built, a section of which runs through our parish, life has become easier for commuters.

In a lovely setting near the river and church is the park, a legacy one could say from the Second World War. During that time, Park Farm was commandeered for open cast coal mining, and afterwards the site was transformed into a park for the people of Polesworth.

🍁 PRESTON BAGOT

Preston Bagot, just to the east of Henley-on-Arden is a small village with an interesting little church.

The church of All Saints stands high on a hill. It is very peaceful there and the churchyard is kept with loving care. Those who are lucky enough to be there at the right moment may see the altar cross set ablaze with light, the architect having designed the window so that at sunset the dying sun strikes directly upon the cross.

The church is 11th to 12th century and is steeped in history. Upon investigation for damp many years ago, two skeletons were found between the outer and inner walls and, after considerable interest and research, were duly given a Christian burial.

Travellers are rewarded after making the steep climb up the narrow church path, with panoramic views in all directions and with the crystal clear air of this high vantage point.

🍁 PRESTON-ON-STOUR

Preston appears in most of the guide books on Warwickshire and words like 'idyllic, tranquil, picturesque, quiet backwater' are always quoted and are absolutely true. But Preston is more than that, it is a living community and has not yet become just a commuter village. It is part of Alscot Estate, and has been in the West family since 1749. Even today most houses and much of the surrounding countryside belong to the present owner, Mrs Emma Holman-West.

The village has a population of just over 100, and a varied cross section of people live here, farmers and farm workers, local craftsmen, past and present employees of the Estate, as well as a smattering of teachers, civil servants, solicitors, retired folk and young mothers. Preston is said to derive its name from 'Priestown', and Alscot Park (the West family mansion) is built on the foundations of an ancient monastery belonging to Deerhurst Priory. The oldest house in the village, whose angle completely defies gravity, is still called the Priest's House, and was said to have been used by the monks conducting services in the church of St Mary.

Take the turning to Preston after crossing the Stour and you find yourself in The Street, with its neat Victorian brick houses on either side, quite a model village in the early 1850s when they were rebuilt. Each has its own outhouse or 'brewhouse' and pig sty at the back, and a yew tree by the front gate. This old tradition is rarely seen these days, and so Preston is rightly proud of its yew trees, the symbol of immortal life. At the end of The Street is the village green, with the church of St Mary on one side and Lockes Farm on the other. The latter is a marvellous old half timbered farmhouse, and is just one of the many lovely old buildings that make up the village. Indeed, there have only been three new houses built in Preston since 1852.

From the green there are two loop roads. The top one leads up past the Old Thatch to Park Farm, the bottom one past labourers cottages and The Dell to Lower Farm. Both farms are very important in the working life of the village and their activities are a constant source of interest throughout the year.

A very old tradition carried out in Preston is the Harvest Supper held in October at the village hall. This dates back to the time when much of the stock had to be killed before the winter months, and today it is still very much a meat meal. Between 80 and 90 villagers sit down at two long candlelit trestles to plates of cold turkey, ham and beef and enjoy a really old fashioned harvest supper with their neighbours. The village hall was formerly the

149

Coronation Hall built by the villagers in 1953 and was replaced in 1999 by a splendid brick-built hall renamed the Three Parishes Millennium Hall.

One of the most delightful things about all these village functions is the age range of those attending – from the very old to the very young all join in. Talking to older members of the village, Preston has certainly changed over the years. For instance in the 1920s Alscot estate used to employ about 30 villagers working at the Park, gardens and farm land, but now that number is drastically reduced. There is no doubt that like most rural communities Preston is changing.

🍁 PRINCETHORPE

No, not a romantic prince, but probably an Anglo-Saxon farmer called Pren. The name has been known for 800 years.

Joseph Elkington of Stretton was awarded £1,000 by Parliament in 1795 for his new land-drainage system. Hitherto, open drains were used in the fields, despite their interference with cultivation. Elkington drained a field in Princethorpe to show how wet marginal land could be made productive – a necessary step in the Agricultural Revolution. The Government hastened with the payment in case all knowledge of his original 1764 discovery died with him as he was in 'precarious health'. From the award was founded the family firm of Elkingtons, the famous silversmiths.

Early in the 20th century the village was much more self-contained and self-sufficient than it is today. Men worked on their own farms and smallholdings or for other farmers including the Priory. An unusual feature of the village was the woman chimney sweep who travelled round the locality carrying her equipment on her bicycle.

Ghost stories are common but strangely none of the ghosts haunted Coffin Walk between Princethorpe and the parish church at Stretton, which traditionally was maintained at five feet, ie the width of a coffin and bearers. This path forks to The

Shoulder of Mutton in Stretton. Perhaps the bearers came back that way!

The outstanding building is the Priory church. Added by Peter Paul Pugin in 1897, its fine red brick tower is a landmark. The site was acquired by a group of French Benedictine nuns from Montargis who in 1792 escaped from the French Revolution, helped by Mrs Fitzherbert, the Prince Regent's wife. The nuns had been forced by a bad storm to land at Shoreham and the Prince himself thoughtfully sent carriages from Brighton for them. He arranged overnight lodging and ordered travelling cloaks for their journey to Norfolk where they had been lent a house. In gratitude, the nuns have ever since sung a daily prayer for the Sovereign.

After several moves, the nuns bought land at Princethorpe in 1832 and settled there in the new building with their school. The bricks were made of clay dug on site and fired nearby. A reservoir built there and later artistically landscaped to resemble a small lake at Montargis was christened Little Switzerland. The building of the Pugin church brought hundreds of sightseers every weekend to watch progress. In 1965 the Benedictine nuns sold the Priory to the Missionaries of the Sacred Heart, who then converted it into the independent Catholic school, Princethorpe College.

The Second World War saw several small factories in the village making supplies for the Forces and Civil Defence. Entertaining the Forces was both a duty and a pleasure. Caravans, spare rooms and even outhouses were crowded with Coventrians seeking relief from the nightly bombing.

The early 1950s were an exciting time in Princethorpe. Roman coins were found near Stoneyford Bridge (previous finds included an Anglo-Saxon brooch and an iron spearhead). The notorious Princethorpe bank robber was thought to have buried his loot by his house in Nun's Wood but nobody has been lucky enough to find that. The new road was made then, so that pedestrians no longer had to dodge into the refuges cut into the steep banks on either side of the old narrow Coventry-Oxford road near The Three Horse Shoes, a defile often known as 'the Khyber Pass'.

The old college farm buildings, the Manor House barns and the Old Manor Farm house and buildings have been converted into accommodation for newcomers to the village, providing homes for at least a further 14 families. Today there is no longer a working farm in Princethorpe, the remaining acreage is farmed by farmers from neighbouring villages and part time smallholders. Princethorpe College and the two hotels provide work for many of the women, but otherwise Princethorpe is now a dormitory village even though many of the old families still live there.

🍁 PRIORS HARDWICK

In common with many ancient villages Hardwick's beginnings remain obscure. It can, however, be said with certainty that Hardwick in the Hundred of Honesberie was one of 24 vills with which Earl Leofric endowed the monastery which he founded in Coventry sometime before 1043. Hardwick is also recorded in the Domesday Book.

Sometime before the Dissolution of the Monasteries the village was destroyed, with subsequent depopulation. The destruction was probably ordered by the Prior of Coventry to provide solitude for the monks and grazing for the flocks of sheep introduced to cater for the wool and meat markets. The site of the deserted village lies behind St Mary's church in the field known as Farm Close. The fishponds are still discernible together with several house platforms and a number of holloways.

After the Dissolution of the Monasteries Sir Edmund and Lady Ursula Knightley were granted the manor. Repopulation began in the late 16th century on the fringes of the former village.

There were at least 20 holders of lands in the parish at this time. They farmed in the open fields, growing barley, oats, wheat, peas, hay and hops, and grazing cattle, horses and sheep. That the Rainbows, Wilkshiers, Gubbins, Sherleys and their neighbours must have worked hard to survive on the heavy clay soil goes without saying. How they took their leisure, if indeed they had

152

any, remains to be discovered.

Spice must surely have been added to life in the village by the visits of the, by all accounts, lively Welsh drovers as they progressed on their way to and from the London markets with their herds of cattle, sheep, pigs or flocks of geese. The ancient Salt Road, used for carrying salt and other commodities from Droitwich to Northampton would doubtless have brought travellers into the settlement.

The old system of open field farming was brought to an end in 1767 with an Act of Parliament dividing and enclosing the land. With the planting of quickthorn hedges to enclose the various parcels of land the present pattern of fields began to take shape. From 1869 on into the early 1900s several small farms were sold, and acquired by one family, marking the beginning of the trend which eventually led to the amalgamation of the majority of land in the parish to form three farms.

One can imagine the effect on the community of the murder of Betsy Handcock. On the night of the 13th November 1872 she was stabbed by her husband, the local pig butcher. Edward Handcock earned himself the dubious distinction of being the last man hanged in Warwick Gaol.

About 172 people now live in the village. The school closed in 1959, the children now depart daily by bus or car to be educated in other places. The vicarage has been sold, the vicar now resides in Priors Marston. The village has no shop or post office, although there is a pub with restaurant, and the beautiful old church of St Mary's. The post office closed in 1993 – Mrs Winn ran it for 40 years and three months. Residents see Hardwick as a tranquil place in which to live, far removed from urban activity, providing solitude without isolation. Only a handful of people find a livelihood in the community, incomes are earned in the surrounding towns, but in an everchanging world today sheep still graze in Priors Hardwick.

🍁 PRIORS MARSTON

Priors Marston lies to the south-east of the county with the village set at the side of a ridge which forms the edge of the Northamptonshire uplands. Fine views to the west can be obtained, with the Malvern Hills in the distance and on very clear days one can see as far as the Cambrian mountains.

The name Priors Marston is from the Anglo-Saxon 'merse' meaning marsh with 'ton' meaning town (or, in this case, village). The Priors was added by the monks of the Benedictine Priory of Coventry after the manor was endowed to them, with 23 others, by Earl Leofric in 1043. It is mentioned in the Domesday Book of 1086 as part of Priors Hardwick, the next parish, but by 1236 was listed on the Priors Terriers as a separate place. However, a settlement was undoubtedly in existence many generations before these dates.

It is set on the very ancient Ridgeway Track with the Jurassic Way nearby. Priors Marston is also situated on the Droitwich to Northampton Salt Road (mentioned in 956) along which salt was carried for tanning and meat preservation. The Welsh Drovers' Road also enters the parish. This runs from the Welsh Borders through to Barnet near London. A High Constable was stationed here to deter highwaymen, as one of the main coaching routes from Warwick to London (via Towcester) also ran through the village. The Oxford canal, opened in 1790, lay just on the boundary of the village.

The parish has been mainly agricultural for hundreds of years with the ridge and furrow method of farming still evident in places. After the dissolution of Coventry Priory in 1539 the manorship passed through several hands until it was granted to Robert, Lord Spencer in 1602 who, with succeeding Spencers, greatly influenced the character of the whole area although the Priors Marston farms were mainly let off to tenants and not actually farmed by them. The general layout of the fields was finally set by The Enclosure Act of 1758, although, with modern farming, a considerable number of hedges have been removed. Earl Spencer is still Lord of the Manor.

The village, which became a conservation area in 1972, is an attractive grouping of stone and brick houses with only minor development occurring up to 40 years ago. Since then, as with practically all other villages, infilling has occurred with varying impact on the village scene. Look out for the houses around the village green. High House was built for Earl Spencer's agent. Hillview, by the War Memorial, was once the workshop of Edward Gardner, a well-known chairman of the Cotswold tradition. Next door, with its tall central chimney, is Westover Farm, once owned by a famous clockmaker called Blenco Churchill (who died in 1764). His clock faces only had one hand.

Walk along the network of blue brick paths that run through the village and note how the friendly church and churchyard form part of the village with its collection of interesting tombstones. There is one for Josiah Key (died 1711), generous local benefactor who was a locksmith to the Court of William III and Queen Anne. His house still exists in the village and a lane is named after him. Nearby you will find the tombstone to Sarah Rainbow, inscribed:

> Here lieth one bereaved of life
> A sober Christian and a loving wife
> Seven sons – to them a mother kind
> She lived to bury three – and four were left behind.

The oldest part of the church is 13th century, the tower was remodelled in 1720 and extensive rebuilding and renovations occurred in 1863.

Records show that a number of stone houses were built around 1650 to 1700 and it is thought that, in addition to farming, the local wool trade and the building of Banbury market and manufacturing helped the prosperity of the village. The Falcon Inn, now a private house, is a very old building and was a calling point for stage coaches. The Holly Bush Inn is also very old, although it has only been a public house since the turn of the 20th century.

With a total population of around 500 the parish has a

modern mix of local town commuters and retired people with very few working on the farms. Over 80 per cent of the parish is now divided into four farms.

Several buildings have now been converted into holiday lets and some houses have become second homes for town dwellers. There are no local industries, and the once brickyard has been developed for housing. The new village hall is a millennium project funded by the local authority, the National Lottery, ACRE and the villagers. The school, closed by the LEA in 1994 was reopened as a charity school, funded by villagers and other organisations. It flourishes, with a nursery opened in 1999.

QUINTON & ADMINGTON

Quinton, originally Queans-town (in Saxon language 'Quean' meant woman), was so-called because it was in the possession of the nuns of Polesworth until the Norman Conquest, when King William granted their rights to Sir Robert Marmion and his heirs.

In 1919 the inhabitants of Quinton, numbering about 300, were employed either on farms or in nearby market gardens. The population had grown to nearly 2,500 by 1990, many working in the nearby Royal Engineers Camp, but with the closure of the camp the number has dropped to around 1,500 with a further 100 living in Admington.

When the Camp was closed in 1998 the army accommodation, both inside and outside the camp area was vacated. The closure affected not only many local people who worked there but also St Swithun's church. Army personnel had carried out much work in the church, including constructing a door between the bell-tower and nave, erecting a board listing previous incumbents and making the iron light fittings.

St Swithun's church is almost 1,000 years old and it is well worth a visit for its many different styles and periods of architecture, its heraldic windows and fascinating history. The most recent addition being a stained glass window in the chancel incorporating the RE badge, a gift of the Army and a reminder of their close involvement for many years.

On a tablet on the front of the old church school is inscribed a text from Ecclesiastes Ch 12, v1–12: 'Remember now thy Creator in the days of thy youth.' The building, which was used by a youth club for several years, has a unique exterior which it is hoped will be retained when it is sold for redevelopment.

The new school, built after the Second World War, is still operational and Quinton retains its village shops and post office. It also has two pubs – The Gay Dog, which used to be a farmhouse and The College Arms, originally owned by Magdalen College, Oxford, and the only pub entitled to carry the College coat of arms.

Magdalen College, the major landowner, has sold off most of the larger houses and cottages; many of the latter have been joined to make larger dwellings. This applies especially to Admington, which remains largely unspoiled. Admington Hall is still privately owned but Quinton House was sold about 50 years ago and is now a nursing home.

❧ RADFORD SEMELE

The name is thought to originate from the 'Red Ford' or the 'Reeded Ford' (possibly over the river Leam), and the name of the Norman landowner in the reign of Henry I, who was Henry de Simely. Hence, the Red (or Reeded) Ford on the land of Simely.

But there is evidence of life in the village long before the reign of Henry I. A flint hand axe and two other flints were found in 1968 – they would have belonged to ancient Britons over 30,000 years ago.

Radford Semele parish lies between Leamington Spa to the west, Offchurch to the north and the Roman Fosse Way to the east. Coins dating back to the Roman period have been found in gardens in the village, so presumably there was habitation here around AD 300. The site of a Roman villa on Pounce Hill Farm, about half a mile west of the Fosse Way, was brought to light in the 1920s.

The oldest building in the village is the church. It is probable that in medieval times the village centred around the church but sometime later, by 1600, the whole village had moved half a mile away. The reason for this is not known, but the church remains isolated from the village.

There may have been a church here before the Norman Conquest, but monks from Kenilworth Priory built, or rebuilt it, in the early 12th century. The only Norman part remaining is the south wall where the typical rubble masonry and a small window can be seen. The tower, which is possibly on older foundations, is thought to be of 15th century construction. Over the centuries the church has undergone alterations and rebuilding. The church interior, as it is seen today, is largely a result of the extensive rebuilding of 1889. In 1998 two new bells were added to the tower to make a ring of six, and a new steel frame fitted to take the six bells; this was partly funded by the Millennium Commission.

Radford Hall was probably built between 1600 and 1620, and contains some fine wood carving, dated 1622, which is believed to have been done by a travelling band of Huguenots. There remains part of an ancient wall, which may have encircled the grounds and may be older than the Hall itself. A fine postern gate, in this wall, is visible from the road. In the early 19th century, the building was rebuilt, with brick covering the original stone. The Hall has recently been converted into several dwellings.

Radford was famous in the area for its ale. This was originally 'home brewed' at Radford Hall, but proved so popular that the Thornley family built a brewery on land opposite the Hall. This flourished from 1900 until takeover and closure in 1969. The site is now occupied by a design company.

There are two thatched houses on the main road through the village near the turn to Offchurch. One of these has an unusual chimney, which divides and then rejoins, with a window in the middle. This is clearly seen on the east end of the house.

The Manor House, opposite the thatched houses, was built around 1800 and has a round tower similar to the one on Edgehill. Considerable additions were made in the late 19th century. It has been divided into four dwellings.

The White Lion, with its thatched roof, is the only pub in the village, and dates back to the 17th century. A number of clay pipes have been found on land to the south of the inn. These pipes date from 1640 to 1710, and were probably thrown on the rubbish tip from the White Lion.

The old village of Radford Semele was situated along the main turnpike road and what is now called Lewis Road. There was considerable expansion in the village after 1956. Prior to this, the population had been between 500 and 600 for over a hundred years. Today the population is around 2,500.

The canal, which passes through the parish, was begun in 1795, and opened in 1800 as the Warwick and Napton Canal. It later became part of the Grand Union Canal. The original narrow locks were widened during the modernisation programme of 1925.

The railway linking Leamington with Rugby was built in 1851, and included a fine skew arched bridge over the canal near the boundary with Offchurch. The railway track was lifted in 1967. Today this part of the railway, and the canal towpath, are popular walks for villagers.

🍁 Radway

Visitors today see in the wooded slopes of Edgehill, scene of a Civil War battle in 1642, a blend of past and present and from the top, a panorama of 12 counties. Also from the top, the Round Tower, built in 1750, watches over Radway from the spot where the king's standard was set up before the battle.

The tower's architect, Sanderson Miller, planted trees below the tower, and was also responsible for the meaningless turrets added to the once beautiful Grange. The Stoneleigh monks were the early owners of the Grange, they demolished the existing building and built the main part of the present house. A well was sunk and fish-ponds were made and stocked. John Washington was the owner during the Battle of Edgehill, kinsman to George

The Round Tower at Radway, built in 1750

Washington, the first President of the USA. Today the Grange still plays a part in the community life.

The parish church, dedicated to St Peter, and the Methodist chapel both celebrated a centenary in 1966. When the old church was demolished, foundations of a previous one were discovered, and the Norman period gargoyles were dug up and incorporated in the tower of the present church. The five bells in the tower are enthusiastically rung on every possible occasion.

Long ago there was a strong association with the Quakers – the old Meeting House is now a private dwelling, and a garden covers the burial ground.

Horses have always been important, in bygone days for work and transport, providing useful local employment. Blacksmith, wheelwright, carrier, saddler, all had a prominent part to play. Now there are more horses than ever before, but used for different purposes. The demand today is for sport and recreation.

An early attempt at education was a 'Dame School' under the patronage of squire and vicar in a cottage at the Grange entrance. In 1851, Charles Chambers of Ivy Lodge, built the school and in 1852 an 'excellent Reading Room', now called the Institute. He left both properties in the care of his cousin, Georgiana. Eventually some Board School regulations were incorporated, and then in 1912 the County Council took over. In 1966 progress dictated that the school be closed, and now the children travel to Tysoe and to Kineton. The school is now a house.

🍁 RATLEY WITH EDGEHILL & UPTON

Ratley was a medieval village, facing south and nestling on the edge of the Cotswolds. It was built on the old Banbury to Stratford road where the pub and the church stand (now known as Featherbow Lane). From AD 1100 to the turn of the 20th century it changed very little due to poor transport facilities. Quarrying was its first industry and provided a livelihood for the inhabitants, while farming was carried out as a means of survival. The local stone is a lovely honey brown with blue flashes and the village keeps its character with dwellings built in this stone. The Hornton stone quarry is at Edgehill and still brings employment to the area. The cutting of the old railway line which carried ironstone by rail through Ratley to the main railway line at Fenny Compton still remains, but due to a fatal accident in 1913 the line was never completed.

Land that has been quarried is being reclaimed and planted out with trees leaving grassy areas in between to encourage wild flowers. It is designated to become a Nature Reserve. In 1971 the old part of Ratley was recognised as a Conservation village and this has helped to keep the character of the village.

A barn which belongs to the village was converted into the village hall in 1937. Previously it had been used as a corn and potato store for the villagers and at one time as a soup kitchen for the very poor. It is now well used for recreational and educational purposes.

The local, The Rose and Crown, was a 'spit and sawdust' pub – one room with beer sold out of a jug until the 1970s, when it was transformed into a modern pub with brasses, beams, open hearth and a restaurant. It is a listed building.

Next door is the old church which in recent years has enjoyed a musical revival with musical events including performances of Handel's *Messiah*. The church has four bells. The first bell was put in in 1677, a tenor bell in 1763, a treble in 1859 and another treble in 1985. Amos John England, now living in a cottage called 'Wayside', followed his grandfather as bellringer and is, according to a previous rector, 'an astonishing one-man act on 3 ropes, pulling with both hands and one foot'.

The village school was built in 1887 but closed in 1976 due to small numbers of children in the village and high costs. The children now travel to Tysoe school, approximately 3 miles away.

Edgehill comes within the Parish boundary and is famous for past events, but mostly for the Civil War battle of 1642, fought underneath the escarpment in the Parish of Radway. Ghost legends and myths of the battle still persist, such as sounds of battle, and sightings of the galloping white charger said to be Prince Rupert's.

Upton House stands a mile away from Edgehill and was built in the 17th century. It is now a National Trust property and brings many visitors and tourists to our village and woods. In the summer there is a typical English scene of white clad figures on the cricket pitch, and in the winter the Warwickshire hunt hold their meet at the House.

🍁 ROWINGTON

Anybody looking for the village of Rowington has a difficult task, for it is a place of scattered hamlets originally established by a group of Saxons of Hwicce heritage. Their leader was 'Hroca' and their settlement 'Hrocingatun' – meaning 'homestead of Hroca's people'. In the Domesday Book this had become 'Rochintone'. The whole area was then covered by part of the Forest of Arden, and thus a typical fragmented woodland village was formed, which is now bisected by the B4439 road to Warwick.

There remain in the parish some substantial timbered old houses, of which Shakespeare Hall is obviously of particular interest. Legend has it that a branch of the Shakespeare family lived here in William Shakespeare's time, and there is ample evidence of Shakespeare farmers in the community for many years. Whether or not they were directly connected with the

Shakespeare Hall

famous bard remains a mystery!

The nearby quarry, now extinct, was once of considerable importance. Rowington stone was used extensively in Warwickshire buildings, notably for St Philip's cathedral, Birmingham, for Baddesley Clinton Hall (NT) and, of course, for the parish church of St Lawrence, which stands dramatically atop the steep hill on the southern approach to the village. Expert opinion considers that the 12th century Norman church was considerably rebuilt in the late 13th century, with further additions being made in the 14th and 15th centuries. These days Rowington shares a rector with the other nearby parishes which comprise the North Ferncumbe group.

Rowington Hall is opposite and appears to be on the site of an earlier manor house. The land around it was at one time a game park for the use of the Abbey and Abbot of Reading, to whom the manor then belonged, and it is marked on old maps as Rowington Park.

Standing as it does on high ground, the village has a strong association with windmills. Long-term residents remember 'Bouncing Bessie' in action on Rowington Green. Mr Boyle was the last miller there – and permanently covered in flour, or at least in the memory of those who recall him. 'Grinning Jenny' is believed to have been a wooden post mill, and 'Tom o' the Wood' was somewhere near the Tom o' the Wood Inn, renamed in 1975 for this reason.

In the recent past the village has been well served by generous benefactors, including the Wilson family of Shakespeare Hall who gave the land on which the village hall now stands. Built in 1949, after much fund-raising and hard work by many members of the community, the hall has recently celebrated '50 years of good times' and is the hub of local activities.

Mr E. L. Edwards was another public spirited resident who, in 1912, purchased the field used for cricket and rented it to the club for a nominal sum. Forty years later his two daughters gave the picturesque ground to the village in trust, and one of the real joys of a summer Sunday afternoon is the sound of bat on ball and a distance shout of 'How's that' – an irresistible temptation to dwellers nearby to sneak over for a sit down and a cup of tea! Mr and Mrs F. S. Ryland (also one time owners of Shakespeare Hall) added to the amenities by funding the adjacent Rowington Working Men's Club building.

Prior to the existence of the village hall, the school was the centre of social as well as educational activity under its popular headmaster, Mr Herbert McWilliams. Fetes and concert parties were his particular passions and provided great village participation and entertainment. The closure of his school in 1984 would have been unthinkable to Mr McWilliams, and was a sad day for everyone. The little shops of the village, the cobbler's hut and the woodsheds near to the schoolhouse have also gone, and so has the legendary Maud Barlow, who succeeded her father and grandfather as landlord of the Cock Horse Inn. 'The Cock' was also the forge and her father was blacksmith as well as landlord.

In the 1960s a local authority development of some 40 houses and elderly person's bungalows increased the population quite considerably and more recently the schoolhouse itself has been converted into an attractive terrace of dwellings. Nevertheless, the Green Belt has so far protected the village from large-scale building and the several working farms are still currently managed by long-standing local families, their custody shaping the surrounding countryside. The Grand Union Canal runs close to the village and the National Trust-administered Stratford-on-Avon Canal also meanders on its way through nearby fields. Both bring holidaymakers from many parts of the world to walk the lanes, to moor up at canalside pubs and to inspect with interest the barrel-roofed lock cottages of the Stratford-on-Avon Canal, which are unique to the area.

Rowington is a very sociable village and the year's unfolding is marked by traditional annual milestones – the Spring and Summer Shows of the Horticultural Society; the Cricket and Tennis Club functions; the village hall May Ball and Christmas Dance; the British Legion Ex-Servicemen's Supper and the 'Old Folks' Summer Outing and Christmas Luncheon each take priority in turn, and combine with the seasonal Festivals of the

Church to bring the community together on a regular basis and ensure that rural life need not be lonely – or dull!

🍁 SALFORD PRIORS

The village lies on the main road between Stratford-upon-Avon and Evesham. Coming over Marridge Hill (many years ago called Marl Ridge) you see to the left the river Arrow gently making its way through the fields to where it joins the Avon. To the right can be seen the hamlet of Dunnington, and straight ahead the tower of the parish church can just be seen through the surrounding trees, a peaceful and pleasant view. The parish consists of the village of Salford Priors with the hamlets of Abbots Salford, Rushford, Irons Cross, Cock Bevington, Wood Bevington and Dunnington.

It is a very old village going back to Saxon times and there are still 13 black and white thatched cottages. The old village name was Salteford Major, with Abbots Salford being Salteford Minor, as they were on the Salt Way from Droitwich. St Mary's Priory Kenilworth came into possession of the village, so it became Priors Salford. Salteford Minor passed into the hands of the Abbot of Evesham and so became Abbots Salford.

The church of St Matthew stands surrounded by fields, said to have grown grapes in the days of the Romans. At the entrance to the church is a lovely Norman doorway, built about 1080. There are Norman arches inside from when the church was extended, lancet windows of the 13th century, and a beautiful Flamboyant window.

One of the most celebrated inhabitants was Valentine Green. Born in 1739, he became a mezzotint engraver to King George III and was also commissioned by the Elector of Bavaria.

Another inhabitant who left his mark was William Perkins who was a tailor. Believing in education, he left money for this purpose, and eventually a school was built in 1860, which is still used and has been extended. In 1900 scholarships were awarded through the Perkins Trust to the Grammar School, this continuing until 1948. The Trust still continues for the benefit of the young people of the area.

In Abbots Salford stands a beautiful building, Salford Hall, now renovated as a hotel. At one time it belonged to John Alderford, whose daughter Margaret married Sir Simon Clark in the 17th century. She died, and there is a large heraldic memorial erected in 1631 to her memory. He later married Lady Dorothy Hay who was the daughter of Thomas Hobson of Cambridge, the carrier and stage coach owner, who became famous for the expression 'Hobson's Choice'. There is a beautiful and unusual memorial to Lady Dorothy in the church. The Hall was also used by nuns from 1807 until 1838, where they started a school for young ladies, and until recent years the house was always referred to as the Nunnery by the local people.

Until the Second World War the parish was self-supporting as there was a wheelwright and carpenter (who was also the undertaker), a blacksmith, cobbler, baker, and dairy farmer. The main occupation for the men was in agriculture, until an engineering works was started by Bomford Bros at Pitchill. The firm of Bomford and Evershed has now expanded to a modern factory beside the Banbrook, where agricultural machinery is exported all over the Continent, and provides employment for many people.

Park Hall, a lovely old house and grounds which has been made into flats and dwelling houses, was the Dower House to Ragley Hall. The Marquis was born here when his parents Lord and Lady Henry Seymour were in residence.

Going up to the Bevingtons, the views are breathtaking. There is an old manor house at Wood Bevington and at Dunnington there is a school built like a small church. Indeed it was used as a school all the week and a church on Sundays until after the Second World War, now it is just the primary school. There is also a very nice Baptist church standing in the middle of the hamlet with once again beautiful views over the surrounding lands.

🍁 SAMBOURNE

Sambourne has been a community for 900 years. Drovers met at 'Sandburne' before making the journey through the ancient forest of Feckenham. In the recent past, small industries, connected with needle making, were based in Sambourne. These, along with a forge, a mill and a small brick kiln, have now disappeared.

Today, Sambourne is a rural community of some 150 houses and 350 inhabitants, surrounded by attractive countryside. It is a peaceful village and although it is close to both Redditch and Studley, it has succeeded in maintaining its identity.

The social centre of the village, if not the geographical centre, is the village green with its war memorial and chestnut trees. The village green is used by the community for village functions and the main 'village' buildings are found here.

The pub is next to the green. The present building, flanked by yew trees, is over 400 years old and replaced an earlier inn. It is a black and white timber-framed structure. Inside, original oak beams and stone floors are welcoming. On the opposite side of the green is the building which housed the village shop and post office. Sadly, like so many other village shops, this has now closed and Sambourne has lost an important meeting place.

Sambourne is part of the widespread parish of Coughton, Sambourne, Spernal, Morton Bagot and Oldberrow. As such, Sambourne does not have a parish church, this being at Coughton. Instead it has a building next to the green which is used for both worship and village meetings. In 1882, villagers raised money to build a meeting place for Sambourne. An area was separated from the main room by a screen. This area stores the lectern and table so that when the screen is removed the room can be used for church services. The building was opened with a service followed by tea and entertainment. Thus, the joint function of the building was established and Sambourne can be proud that past residents built such a useful building.

Houses in Sambourne are a pleasing blend of old and new. Most are situated to the north-west of the green. There are several old, part-timbered houses including Yew Tree Cottage (the green) and Crossroads (Sambourne Lane). An attractive terrace of cottages on Sambourne Lane is maintained by the Sambourne Trust, a village charity dedicated to the welfare of villagers.

The population of Sambourne is made up of a broad spectrum of people. Some families can claim to have lived in the village for generations. Others are newcomers. Various village organisations, the church, the WI, the Parish Council and hopefully, in the future, a 'community society', draw the community together.

🍁 SECKINGTON

Although a very small hamlet, Seckington possesses a disproportionate wealth of history.

In AD 757 King Ethelbald of Mercia (and ruler of all England south of the Humber) was killed here, either murdered by his own thanes or killed in battle by his successor, Beornred.

From the main road (B5493) one can see a well preserved Norman motte and bailey. Seckington appears in the Domesday Book. The Manor was held by the Burdett family from the time of Henry II (reigned 1154–1189), and passed down in the direct male line from Edward III's reign (1327–1377) until 1919. The church contains a fine Elizabethan monument to Robert Burdett (died 1603) and his wife. It also depicts their two sons and two daughters. In 1316 a Robert Burdett held the Manor jointly with Gerald de Sekyndon, whose descendants, now called Seckington (like the village), still maintain connections with the village of their ancestors.

Another family of interest was the Washington family who owned and occupied two properties here during the reign of Henry VIII. Sycamore Cottage, although rebuilt, is thought to have been one of these. George Washington, first President of the United States, was a descendant of these Washingtons. His great-grandfather, John Washington, settled in Virginia in 1657 and may have been from Seckington. The coat of arms of the family used to be in the church.

Seckington Church

The present village is principally a farming community consisting of four old farms (three working), farm cottages, a Victorian Gothic Old Rectory and a small number of modern houses.

🍁 SHOTTERY

Many people hearing the name Shottery would inevitably think of Shakespeare and without question the Bard has had a great deal to do with the present popularity of Shottery – a 'must' on the visitors' lists. But the history of Shottery goes much further back than the 16th century when Shakespeare was born. Among the earliest relics to have been found here are fossils of the skeletons of echinoderms – plant-like invertebrates – which may be seen in the museum at New Place (Nash's House). Also in the museum is a collection of Middle Stone Age flints dating from 8000–3500 BC. There is also evidence that the Romans came to Shottery, as three Roman coins were found at the foot of Bordon Hill, and the Alcester Road is also part of a Roman road.

Shottery is featured in the Domesday Book and in 1182 accounted for an acreage of approximately 800 acres which would support about 70 people. By the late medieval period there were two great houses in Shottery. The Manor House, now Shottery Girls' Grammar School on the east side of Shottery Brook and The Hewlands, a large farmhouse later to be known as Ann Hathaway's Cottage on the west. The houses in Tavern Lane were associated with the Manor House and those in the Hamlet with The Hewlands.

There were a number of housing developments in the 1930s and since the end of the Second World War extensive building developments have been made.

In the field of education, it seems there was a Dame School provided by a charity founded by Thomas Eden of Weston-sub-Edge in 1733 for 21 boys and girls aged 5–9 years. They were to be taught spelling, reading, to recite the Catechism and sewing for the girls. For this the Dame was paid £9.2s. a year. Books, Bibles

171

and Testaments were provided by the charity. When the Education Act of 1870 was passed, this amount of schooling was considered inadequate and a new school was built – the actual building being a tithe barn transported from Redditch, donated by the Rev A. H. Williams of Alcester. The school was opened on 2nd December 1870.

Until 1871, it is assumed that Shottery villagers worshipped at Holy Trinity, the parish church of Stratford. There was a Nonconformist chapel near The Bell Inn from about 1833. This is now the Elim Pentecostal church. In 1870 land was given by the Priest in Charge at Bishopton church for the building of a church at Shottery.

During the 1990s additional funds were raised to extend the Shottery St Andrew's church building, and the new hall is in constant use by many local community associations.

Further local fund raising brought about the opening on 28th October 1999 of the new Shakespeare Hospice, which offers a wide range of palliative care for patients and support for their families.

After the end of the Second World War a Memorial Hall was built in Hathaway Lane, and this serves as a venue for many and varied activities and organisations. One of these is a Women's Institute market which meets on Friday mornings where an excellent selection of high quality produce is on sale.

At the end one must return to Shakespeare. It is his fame which has brought Shottery world wide recognition and many thousands of visitors, including Royalty and Heads of State, every year to visit Ann Hathaway's Cottage, now in the care of the Shakespeare Birthplace Trust. Cottages built near to Ann Hathaway's Cottage have been improved in recent times and their colourful gardens contribute a floral welcome, while nearby tearooms and restaurants provide sustenance and cheer before the visitors return to their hotels or homes.

❦ SHREWLEY, LITTLE SHREWLEY, HATTON & HASELEY

On the fringe of Shakespeare Country, in the heart of England, lie the Warwickshire villages of Shrewley, Little Shrewley, Hatton and Haseley.

Little Shrewley is a hamlet of attractive old and new houses and was once the 'hub' of the area, with a pin factory, a coal yard, grinding mill and large nursery garden, all of which ceased functioning after the Second World War. The mill is now a craft centre, specialising in pine furniture, bookbinding, soft furnishings, etc. A 'village pound' still exists, used for storing scrap metal during the war – it now awaits restoration.

Shrewley Common, part of the benefice with Hatton and Haseley, was merely an area of open land in Little Shrewley's heyday! A history of transport is its heritage. On the western boundary the M40 motorway of six lanes runs in a deep cutting, with the old Great Western Railway also in a deep cutting alongside, this being the Birmingham to Marylebone, London, railway line, built circa 1896. Nearer the village runs the Grand Union Canal through a tunnel built in 1798.

In the 1950s a circus had its winter quarters three-quarters of a mile from Shrewley. The long straight road through the village was ideal for the daily exercising of the performing elephants. The local baker, Mr Hobley, having left his delivery van door open, found the entire contents devoured by the appreciative animals!

The Independent chapel is now a dwelling house close by the excellent family-run post office, general store, newsagent, off-licence, etc. At the west end of the village stands the Durham Ox, a popular village pub set in a 17th century building with a long history as a hostelry.

The village hall superseded the old rustic 'Hut' in the 1960s. With a large car park it is a comfortable, cheerful community centre for the village and district. Many organisations use it, including Shrewley WI. An annual flower show is held in September.

Shrewley has a flourishing marina on the Grand Union Canal by Hatton Station, also a lake for local fishermen at Tunnel Barn Farm in the village.

In the 1960s a Roman settlement was discovered when homes were built on the 'Strawberry Patch'. Artefacts from the exploration are in Warwick Museum.

Hatton is well-known for its 21 locks at a stretch of two and a quarter miles up to Hatton Hill, where boatmen can take refreshment at the Waterman Inn. Hatton Country World, the largest collection of crafts in the country, is a unique blend of shopping and leisure made from 19th century farm buildings, complete with a cafe-bar. A farm park, with rare animals, and a nature trail to Hatton Locks attract many visitors.

The A4177 passes Holy Trinity church with its 16th century tower – the site was used for Saxon worship. The church is in the process of providing extra facilities for all worshippers and visitors.

The Central and Edward VII hospitals have been converted into flats and a new village of 600 houses have been erected in their beautiful grounds. The village school, after some anxious deliberations, is now confident of its future.

St Mary the Virgin, Haseley's beautiful small church, is indeed old. The nave is almost certainly Norman, the chancel is 13th century and the tower was added in the 15th century. The tomb of Clement Throckmorton, 1573 lies in a square bay on the south side of the church. Some religious medieval paintings have been revealed during renovations. Haseley Manor is now a business centre and Haseley House is now a hotel.

The villages are surrounded by undulating countryside with pleasant pastoral views.

🍁 SHUSTOKE

The village of Shustoke covers just over 2,000 acres, and the population is in the region of 500 people. It lies about three miles from Coleshill, on the Nuneaton road.

It is a rural area, though some local farms have now ceased working, a large amount of the land and property belonging to Sir William Dugdale of Blyth Hall (also of Merevale Hall, Atherstone).

Shustoke is mentioned in the Domesday Book as Scotscote, and there are numerous other spellings in old documents and records.

The parish church of St Cuthbert lies about one mile above the village. There was a church in Saxon times, later replaced by a more substantial building of the Norman period, and again a further replacement in the 14th century, which was later completely altered in the Victorian era. That church was irreparably damaged by a fire after having been struck by lightning in 1886, and 1987 saw the centenary of its restoration. The most famous feature of the church is undoubtedly the tomb of the renowned antiquary, Sir William Dugdale, ancestor of the present Sir William and author of *The Antiquities of Warwickshire*. He was born at what is now known as 'The Old Rectory' in Shawbury Lane.

Near to the church are five almshouses, part of the cottages being on the site of the former village school. These are administered under the Huntbach Trust. Until the Plague in 1650, the village was situated near to the church, but people then moved away and built dwellings which formed the nucleus of the present village.

The local school takes children up to the age of 11, not only from Shustoke but from the surrounding villages. It is situated in a very pleasant spot.

The local pub, The Plough, is nearby, and in addition to the regulars one may on occasion see a group of ramblers who have come out to Shustoke for a breath of fresh air and a bit of healthy exercise.

Next to the pub is the Village Pound in which sheep were penned ready for collection for market years ago, and any stray animals were shut in there awaiting collection by their owners. The structure of the Pound was restored by the Parish Council in 1975.

The local post office and stores (built about 1740), where, in addition to having a friendly chat with the proprietor, one could also purchase almost any commodity one could name, has unfortunately now closed and reverted to a private house. The post office is today run from another private dwelling.

Not far from the village centre is Shustoke Reservoir which, with the reservoir in the adjoining parish of Whitacre, and Whitacre Water Works, supplies water to bulk storage reservoirs at Coventry and Nuneaton. There is an enthusiastic sailing club which is based at the reservoir, and anglers also spend many happy hours sitting on the banks fishing for trout.

🍁 SHUTTINGTON

Shuttington is a small residential village of mainly 19th and 20th century buildings, standing high on a hill overlooking Alvecote Pools Nature Reserve. It has more ancient origins however: it was mentioned in the Domesday survey, and the little Norman church was once a chapel to Alvecote Priory.

In the churchyard is buried an 18th century record breaker! Thomas Spooner was the fattest man in England, weighing 40 stone 9 lbs, and measuring 4 feet 3 inches across the shoulders. Such was his size that he could only get around by pony and trap, but his bulk saved his life when, during an argument, he was stabbed and his fat prevented the wound being fatal.

The public house, The Wolferstan Arms is named after the landowning family of nearby Statfold Hall. There is also a village shop, a fine village hall and a playing field.

🍁 SNITTERFIELD

The village lies halfway between Stratford-upon-Avon and Warwick. Its origins are obscure but there is thought to have been a settlement as early as Celtic times, and certainly by the time of the Domesday Book there was a flourishing community. The earliest recorded name was Snytenfeld (in Anglo Saxon 'place of snipe') because the bottom lands of the village, now drained by the Sherborne Brook, were at one time the haunt of snipe, being very boggy. They still are in wet weather, but alas the snipe have gone although there are still herons, and reputedly kingfishers, though the latter are rarely seen. The name was corrupted to Snitfeld and later to its present form.

The village used to be the centre of a thriving agricultural community, with several large farms and most of the villagers employed in farmwork and allied crafts. Gradually the way of life altered until the Second World War saw the end of the varied trades, such as hurdlemaker, blacksmith, saddler and wheelwright which had formerly made the village a self-sufficient farming enclave.

There was even, during the Victorian era, a village brick-kiln and local bricks were extensively used when the Philips family, who virtually owned the village for 100 years from 1816, rebuilt or improved many of the houses.

Today, with modern transport, the neighbouring towns of Stratford-upon-Avon and Warwick are so easily accessible that there is no longer the need for local facilities. The surviving shop, the Snitterfield Stores, does a thriving trade and fortunately there is still the doctors' surgery and dispensary. The post office, however, has closed.

Probably the most famous farmer in local history was Richard Shakespeare, the grandfather of the Bard, who farmed land near the church which he rented from John Arden of Wilmcote, whose daughter Mary married Richard's son John. If only they had stayed here instead of moving to Stratford shortly before William's birth, what a different village this might have become. As it was, the farm was carried on by a ne'er-do-well brother Henry (known to William Shakespeare as 'Uncle Harry') who appears to have been a sore trial both to his father and to his more prosperous brother John.

There is an early Tudor house still standing just beyond the church which is claimed by some to have been the Shakespeare house but this is not certain, and from contemporary records it seems more likely to have been in a different part of the village, probably demolished long ago. There are, however, still a number of genuine Tudor houses remaining in the village, most in private occupation and in better repair than the alleged Shakespeare house. One of them has the additional interest of a ghost! This is reputed to be a soldier, mortally wounded at the Civil War battle of Edgehill who managed to make his way to Snitterfield, but died in the house.

Apart from the Tudor and Jacobean architecture there are two other main types of houses in the village – the Philips houses referred to earlier, which are all in the same distinctive brick and stone style, and many post-war houses, including a fairly extensive council estate.

The completion of the Stratford Northern by-pass, which runs right across the southern edge of the village, destroyed the beautiful tree-lined road known as Kings Lane (because Prince Charles, later King Charles II, is reputed to have fled along it when escaping after his defeat at Worcester). Although the nature of the village has changed somewhat due to the A46 by-pass and the opening of the M40, the village has attracted younger families, which has helped keep open and develop a nursery school and junior school.

❧ SOUTHAM

Although there is no documentary evidence relating to Southam before AD 998, Roman coins discovered during the 19th century in the churchyard and Bury Orchard indicate the probability of a Roman settlement around AD 250–350.

The first documentation is a Charter of King Ethelred the Unready which gave Southam to Leofwine, father of Leofric (husband of Lady Godiva) in 998. Southam is also recorded in the Domesday Book of 1086. The ownership of Southam passed from Leofwine to his son, who bestowed it upon the Prior of Coventry in 1047.

Southam's chief claim to historical fame rests in events immediately prior to the Civil War in 1641, when Charles I is said to have passed through the town. Apparently he was not made welcome and the churchwardens refused to ring the bells. The furious king had the church doors locked until they paid a fine of 13 shillings and 4 pence. However, the stubborn bellringers still refused to ring the bells to wish him 'Godspeed' on his departure, so he sent his footmen back to levy another fine of 5 shillings.

King Charles later returned to Southam and is said to have slept at the Manor House on Market Hill before the Battle of Edgehill. Not to be outdone, the Roundheads also came to the town, and Cromwell himself was here in 1645 with 7,000 troops. However, although battles raged nearby, Southam was not again to become involved in the fighting.

Until the year 1820 four annual fairs took place in Southam. The most important was the Charter Fair, established in 1257 to be held on the Vigil Feast and morrow of St Peter and St Paul. By far the most popular fair was the 'Show Fair' held on the Monday of the first week in June. This included a Lady Godiva Procession probably to commemorate the handing of Southam by Leofric and Lady Godiva to the Monks of Coventry.

St James' parish church was built in perpendicular style in the 16th century. In the tower there is a peal of eight bells. The pulpit is late 16th century.

In 1818 Mr Henry Tilley Smith established an infirmary for eye and ear disorders. The dispensary cottage dated 1840 is no longer in existence but a stone surmounted by an urn is situated near the site, in front of The Stoneythorpe Hotel on the Warwick road, to commemorate the first Provident Dispensary in the country.

The Holywell, according to Arthur Mee's *Warwickshire* is 'Holywell that never freezes and a street that always pleases'. It is thought that the waters from the well were regarded as a cure for eye ailments.

☘ STOCKINGFORD

Stokeyingford, Stokeford or Stooking Lane are names given to land which has been enclosed from wild land since medieval times. The word 'stocking' means stocking up of woodlands or wastelands, and preparing for cultivation. The area which embraces Stockingford at one time was part of the Forest of Arden.

The word 'Ford' means a stream and such a ford existed from a short distance beyond Stockingford station.

A site in Stockingford with woodlands and arable land was granted in 1143 by Earl Robert le Bossu and William de Newmarch to the Canons of St Mary de Pre of Leicester. The Canons had a chapel here by grant of Geoffrey de Turville. The Manor of Stockingfold may be identified with these messuages, and a mill and other land were granted in 1280 by Hugh de Lilleburn to his son Hugh.

In 1898 several acres of glebe land were sold, and as there was a demand for housing accommodation, building began in Church Road and Haunchwood Road. The allotment association was formed and provided 360 allotments. St Paul's church was built on Paddiford Common and consecrated in 1824.

In 1904 oil lamps were discarded and gas lighting was put in. The church was the first public building in England to be lit with the inverted gas mantles.

The main industries in Stockingford were the coal mines and brickyards, which sadly are now all closed, also the Stockingford railway station. In 1887 another pit was working in the Chapel End district which was then included in the Stockingford parish. This pit was termed 'Drybread' on account of the poor pay of the miners.

The Round Towers are north of Arbury Hall and the southern end of Church Road and form the main entrance to Arbury Hall. They are in fine preservation and built of local stone. There is an embattled gateway on either side of which are the residences of the two gatekeepers.

Mary Ann Evans (George Eliot) was born at South Farm on the Arbury Estate. A bronze statue of her was made at the nearby studio of John Letts of Astley, and placed in Newdigate Square in Nuneaton town centre in 1986.

The last Monday in June was a big day in Stockingford. The church and chapels held their Sunday School treats. St Paul's church members processed round the parish with banners and bunting and singing hymns. After tea in the church school, games and races were held in Mr Burdett's field, and every child was given a penny bun. The local brass band headed the procession and played music in the field at night.

🍁 STOCKTON

The first mention of Stockton, which means 'Stump Enclosure', appears in records dated 1272.

It remained a tiny farming hamlet until the discovery of clay and lime in the vicinity. The development of cement and lime industries in the 18th and 19th centuries has had the most influence on the village. Housing was provided for employees and the village increased in numbers.

The industry was sold to Nelson Cement Works early in the 19th century. With the profits the church was renovated and the remaining money was used to employ a Church of England school teacher. A stone house, originally a stable, served as a schoolroom for the local children. By 1824, 33 boys and 19 girls were benefiting from an education. The present day school was built in 1906 and is still in use today as a 'first' school.

During the excavation of the blue lias pit just outside Stockton in 1898, an almost perfect fossil of an ichthyosaurus was found 30 feet below the surface. It lay flat, face down with its paddles spread either side of its body and tail curved to the side, length 19 feet 5 inches. Its age is estimated at 20 million years. The dinosaur was carefully removed and could until recently be seen in the Natural History Museum.

At the turn of the 20th century a rector took up the living in Stockton and his eccentric behaviour is still a topic of conversation today. Archdeacon Colley, as he insisted on being called, although the title had lapsed when he retired from an archdeaconate in the South African diocese of Natal, could be seen wearing his mitre and gown at all times. To encourage children to attend services Archdeacon Colley would play a cornet at the gate of the church each Sunday and in the front pew he had installed a dulcimer for them to play during the hymns.

Perhaps the most unusual act performed by this eccentric rector was the building of his own glass topped coffin. The coffin was kept for many years in his study in the rectory where the children preparing for confirmation would use it as a seat.

A real character of the village was Mr Charles Gardner, well-known all over the world for his wood turning. His first lathe was improvised from an old treadle sewing machine and a car gear box.

Accompanied by his wife, he began to attend the Royal Shows. Invitations followed to attend fairs all over the country, Ireland and Scotland included. It was at the Royal Show that he met many members of the Royal family, including the Queen Mother, Princess Anne and Princess Alexandra. An elephant carved for the Duke of Gloucester's collection, a salad bowl for Princess Alexandra and egg cups for her children were among his royal commissions. Field-Marshal Montgomery received a cheese platter made by Mr Gardner.

The types of wood used were of great significance to Mr Gardner. He knew the origins and type of each piece, many pieces coming from his own garden. His famous model fair roundabout embodies 78 varieties of wood.

Master craftsman Neville Neal, born and bred in Stockton, has been working with wood since he left school at the age of 14. Now his graceful cottage chairs with their slender legs, tall ladder backs and comfortable rush seats are in great demand all over the world. The rushes are collected at the end of July from the upper river Leam near Leamington Hastings, they are then hung to dry to last through the winter. The ash wood used is especially chosen from local timber.

🍁 STONELEIGH

Stoneleigh is steeped in history – a thousand years of development on the banks of the river Sowe which is crossed by Rennie's beautiful bridge of eight arches built in the 19th century.

Stoneleigh Abbey is situated in parkland one mile south of the village across fields which now form the Royal Showground.

Stanlei, as it was called once, lay deep in the Forest of Arden. Now some great oaks still standing in the park are all that remain. Stoneleigh was a royal manor until the reign of Henry I, with its own Hundred Court on Motslow Hill, named from 'moot' or meeting place. Its quarry provided the stone for the church and almshouses.

Through the centuries the village reflected changing times and fortunes. By the time of the Domesday Survey, the manor possessed two mills and 4 miles of woodland in which the king owned the feeding for 2,000 hogs. Later, the living was given to the monks of Kenilworth until the Reformation.

In 1561, Sir Thomas Leigh, Lord Mayor of London, who rode before Elizabeth to her coronation, bought the estate from the Crown. His daughter, Alice, who survived him, married Sir Robert Dudley, illegitimate son of the Queen's favourite, Earl of Leicester. He spent many years trying to prove the legitimacy of his birth but without success. An embittered man, he went to Italy with Elizabeth Southwell – maid of honour to the Queen. Meanwhile Alice, who was created a Duchess in her own right in 1644, was left with her four daughters to administer her estates. She consoled herself by helping the poor and needy. She built the almshouses with their quaint roofs and double rows of high chimneys.

The village changed little over the next four centuries with the Norman church, famous for its Romanesque chancel arch and apostle font, in the meadows by the river, the Parsonage close by. The smithy, only occasionally in use today, stood on the green beside a spreading chestnut tree. A handsome Elizabethan manor house stands proudly overlooking the church meadows where cattle still graze. The school, which was converted from the courthouse, closed in 1975 and has now been converted into luxury flats. The village club was first a gaol, then a coach house where Lord Leigh's coach was kept while he was at church, before becoming a Reading Room.

Most of the property was let to people who worked at the Abbey

183

and the community was that of a large family with Lord Leigh keeping a fatherly eye over all.

In the 19th century there was a thriving pub called The Stoneleigh Arms in what is now known as Forsythia Cottage, where lads from Coventry would cycle at weekends to enjoy the local brew. Their bicycles would be lined four deep against the bank. One Sunday morning about 1890 when Cordelia, daughter of Lord William Leigh was passing by, the lads called and whistled after her. When Lord William heard this he was so horrified that he ordered the pub to be closed and expressed his wish that there should never be another in the village – which explains the absence of one to this day.

About this time the mill on the Sowe was converted into the village co-operative run by Jo Morris who was not only butcher and baker but also transport operator. He had a covered horse-drawn wagon which left the village at 8.30 am each Friday to take people to Coventry. Three people would sit either side while chickens and occasionally a pig were in the centre. Their destination was The Three Tuns in Hertford Street; it returned promptly at midday.

Many of these traditions began to disappear after the Second World War when two new estates were built and people from outside came to live in Stoneleigh. The largest change to the old way of life took place rapidly after 1979 when Lord Rupert Leigh died and large sums of money had to be found for death duties and to restore the Abbey.

As cottages became vacant they were sold on the open market. Old family names which had existed in the village for generations began to disappear as the young people could not afford these properties. The shop and the post office closed and now life revolves round the Village Hall and the Club.

The old order has gone for ever, but new traditions are evolving, such as the annual round of the village each Boxing Day by the Coventry Society of Mummers performing the Stoneleigh Play.

❦ STRETTON ON DUNSMORE

For over a thousand years there has been a community in Stretton on Dunsmore. Despite its location close to the Roman Fosse Way, evidence indicates that the founders of the first village were most probably migrating Anglo-Saxons. The name is undoubtedly Anglo-Saxon, being formed from the words *straet tun on dun mor*, meaning 'village on the road on the high ground'.

A number of well-restored cottages are still grouped around the pretty village green and along the stream which crosses it. Several survive in traditional 16th century black and white designs. With its double gabled front and prominent position, Moor Farm is Stretton's most notable timber-framed house and was extended over the 16th and 17th centuries. In its north-west wing is a room where the Manor Court was said to have been held, with a lock-up in a room below.

The Manor House which now stands opposite the church replaced a manor house of the medieval period once located near the village green. This was in ruins by the 19th century but its position is clearly shown on 18th century maps. Even today stone from the old manor can be seen at the bottoms of walls of nearby cottages and the orchard behind the church is all that remains of the old manor house gardens.

The 19th century added a number of imposing buildings and a fine church dominates the pleasant scene. The present church, designed by Thomas Rickman in 1835 in a Gothic Revival style, replaced an earlier one dating back to the 12th century. Evidence of this can still be seen in the churchyard.

Two traditional inns, the Shoulder of Mutton and the Oak and Black Dog, thrive near the green. They are the last of some nine inns which once provided comfort for travellers passing along the old London to Holyhead road across the wild Dunsmore Heath, where highwaymen roamed.

Near the junction with the Fosse Way, the modern road is still an avenue of trees originally planted in 1740 by the second Duke of Montagu. His vision of 'The Long Avenue', stretching as far as

London, earned him the name 'John the Planter'. Sadly, he died before he could complete his project, which stopped only a few miles away at Dunchurch.

Rural traditions, including an annual May Day celebration, have been encouraged and retained but perhaps the most significant local tradition still observed is the collection of Wroth Silver on a nearby hill. In a ceremony which dates back over 800 years, representatives of villages in the 'Knightlow Hundred', one of the four divisions of the county in the 12th century, gather before sunrise on November 11th. As dawn breaks, pennies are cast into the hollow Knightlow Stone as payment to the Lord of the Hundred, currently the Duke of Buccleuch. The company then retire to a local hostelry for breakfast, speeches and poetry reading. As a final flourish, clay pipes are offered to smoke after the loyal toast. The original purpose of the ceremony is thought to be a form of tax paid to the local lord for grazing rights and to ensure safe passage across his land.

With sympathetic modern housing development, today's village is a combination of old and new, with many young families injecting new vigour into a friendly and active community which is proud to have survived for more than a millennium.

🍁 STUDLEY

The main road through Studley is the Roman Ryknild Street – now the A435. The A435 is also called the Alcester Road and together with Bromsgrove Road and Station Road forms the Studley triangle. Most of the village lay within this triangle, with its green centre, until recent times. Post-war housing estates have spread beyond it, but the green heart is now a school and public playing fields.

Although mentioned in the Domesday Book, only a few ancient buildings survive. One certainly could not call Studley a pretty village but it has a charm all of its own. The river Arrow flows gently by the lovely old church. It has a mill and a castle and a manor house now called Mountbatten House – headquarters of the Royal Life Saving Society.

Studley College, called locally the 'New Castle', was built in 1834 as the home of the Goodricke family, and was until recent years a well known horticultural college for ladies. It is now British Leyland's marketing centre.

Studley is also known for needle-making. Needle Industries' Studley factory is the largest producer of needles in Britain. Traditionally, needles and fishing tackle were made in small factories or 'shops' built behind some of the older houses. In the 1930s most of the small firms were united in Entaco and the small workshops were closed.

One strange thing about Studley – it has 13 pubs! There are also three licensed clubs and two more pubs in Studley Parish at Mappleborough Green.

Older residents remember Foster's little red vans – 'a shop at your door'. These travelled far and wide to isolated farms and villages taking hard-ware, a hundred and one necessities for the home and garden. They once featured in the National Geographic Magazine.

With great local efforts at fund-raising the swimming pool and village hall were built in recent years. The Youth Centre, Health Centre, Library and Fire Station have all increased local facilities, not to mention Entaco Sports & Social Club, built soon after the Second World War.

🍁 TANWORTH-IN-ARDEN

Tanworth ('in-Arden' was added in the 19th century for postal convenience) was believed to be Anglo-Saxon, derived from Tanewotha, the thane's 'worth', or estate. Originally a clearing in the Forest of Arden and hunting ground of the Earls of Warwick, it is now a picturesque village with a friendly atmosphere which attracts many visitors.

The village is set in lovely Warwickshire countryside, still dotted with working farms, some of which have their origins in the 12 moated farm houses which were known in the parish in

Umberslade Hall, Tanworth-in-Arden

early medieval times. In the area is the ancient Codborough Barn; the Danzey windmill which is said to have been in use until the middle of the 19th century is now restored and grinds corn at the Avoncroft Museum. Several residents are still employed in farming and allied occupations but the majority now work outside the village at all levels of industry and business.

In the recent past several Tanworth men have earned respect for their expertise, notably Arthur Lewis, internationally renowned breeder of Shire horses; Robert and Alfred Summers, able engineers and millwrights whose skills were sought nationally; and fine carving by Mr Terry is still to be found in many homes.

Today, Tanworth-in-Arden has a garage, a post office with general store, and an off licence, where once there were several thriving shops and small businesses. Several homes retain names which indicate their former use. The Doctor's House, the Old Boot

Shop, the Bankhouse which was Burman's Bank in the 18th century, the School House which is still occupied by a teacher from the village school, the Old Work House which was built before 1834 when such provision became compulsory, and the Butts. The heart of the village lies round the triangular green with the war memorial and a young chestnut tree which in time should acquire the stature and character of the one it replaced, which was planted to celebrate Queen Victoria's Jubilee.

First mentioned in the 12th century, the church of St Mary Magdalene still flourishes today, its tower a landmark for miles around. Noted among the vicars are the Rev Phillip Wren, great-grandson of the architect, and Rev Robert Fulwode whose 1341 bequest made provision for 'breade and ale' at an 'annual obit for the Ryngars'. They were clearly as much appreciated then as now for they make a fine sound under Jim Corbett who has been Captain of Ringers for 40 years. The Bell on the Green is the one remaining public house and council houses now stand on the Bell Field which for many years was the home of the Annual Flower Show.

There always has been and still is, great demand for homes in the Whitehead Almshouses. The original four houses were presented to the vicars of Tanworth and Ullenhall in 1873. In addition a complex of a further eight flats was opened in 1987. The Trust now operates its own Housing Association but the conditions of residency remain almost identical to those laid down originally. A thriving Church Primary School is still partially maintained by the Tanworth Educational Foundation, which has its roots in charitable donations of land and money made over several centuries. Chairman of the Foundation is F. D. Muntz who is Lord of the Manor of Tanworth and also holds the living of the parish church.

Mr Muntz is the present owner of Umberslade Park, in the centre of which is the Hall, home of the Archer family for many centuries. At the end of the 17th century Andrew Archer rebuilt the Hall, but in 1850 it was bought by the Muntz family, who lived here until the 1950s. It has now been converted into luxury flats. In the grounds is an obelisk built in 1749 by Thomas Archer, probably to commemorate his elevation to the peerage. It is from the Archer family that Tanworth claims its most famous resident, Sir Simon Archer, a renowned antiquarian who initiated work on *The Antiquities of Warwickshire* ultimately compiled by Sir William Dugdale.

❧ TEMPLE GRAFTON

> Piping Pebworth
> Dancing Marston
> Haunted Hillborough
> Hungry Grafton
> Dodging Exhall
> Papist Wixford
> Beggarly Broom
> Drunken Bidford

Temple Grafton is situated five miles to the north-west of Stratford-upon-Avon (off the A422). It is still a peaceful, unspoilt village, despite the recent increase in through traffic due to the Stratford northern by-pass opened in 1987. The village's name is said to derive from the Knights Templars and Knights Hospitallers who once owned the church. Why the village was called 'hungry' is not known but it has been suggested that in Shakespearean times, when the verse above is said to have been written, the land was not very fertile and provided only a poor living for the farming community.

Temple Grafton is one of the villages with a claim to be considered as the place where William Shakespeare was married, but there is no conclusive evidence for this.

Major changes took place in the village between 1855 and 1875. A new Baptist chapel was built. In 1874 Temple Grafton Court was built on the site of the former Manor House by J. W. Carlile who also rebuilt St Andrew's church and provided the village with a new school. Several cottages and a vicarage were also built during these years. There were no further big changes

The village of Temple Grafton

until, between the wars, houses in Croft Lane were built.

Today farming continues to be an important activity but in the years since the Second World War there have been many changes in farming methods, the type of crops produced and in the use of farm buildings and land – all of which have had a profound effect on the appearance of the village and on the life of the community. Farm buildings have been converted into dwellings, one farm now offers bed and breakfast, arable land has given way to large fields, and many hedgerows and wooded areas have disappeared. With mechanisation less labour is needed on the farms and traditional jobs and trades associated with farming have almost disappeared. Most villagers now commute to the local towns.

Temple Grafton and its close neighbour, Ardens Grafton, were once largely self-supporting with a bakery, a grocer, a cider press, a malt house and a blacksmith. People are now totally dependent on shops in the local towns. The post office/general store finally closed down in 1987.

The village school continues to play a vital role in community life and draws children from several neighbouring villages.

The cricket club, founded over a hundred years ago, is still flourishing and continues to play on the original cricket ground at Grafton Court.

However great the social and economic changes, the scenic beauty of the area remains. Temple Grafton and Ardens Grafton lie along a ridge of hills and command superb views of the countryside to the west with the Malvern hills just visible in the distance, and to the south-east, over the Avon valley towards the Cotswolds.

🍁 TREDINGTON

Tredington is a village with a population of approximately 502 situated on the A3400 between Stratford-upon-Avon and Shipston-on-Stour, with the Roman Fosse Way lying to the west.

The earliest reference to Tredington in AD 757 calls it Tredincgtun. By AD 964 the name had become Tyrdintun. The name is believed to have originated from the farmstead or village of Tyrdda.

The dominating feature is the church with its golden spire being a landmark for miles around. It was built in AD 961 and dedicated to St Gregory. There are traces of Norman and Saxon stonework and also the remains of bullets in the vast oak door, reputed to have been left by the Roundheads during their fight with the Royalists.

At the time when the starch factory and two mills employed many of the villagers, there was a butcher's shop, a bakery, a wheelwright and a blacksmith, but now there is only one friendly general store with a post office.

There is a story related by the grandparent of a local resident that, at the turn of the 20th century, there lived an old lady in a cottage on the main road, who had witch's powers. On one occasion the coalman refused to leave a bag of coal because previous supplies had not been paid for. She pleaded: 'Jus' leave me one bag to last I thro' the week.' When he still refused she said, 'If yo' don't leave me a bag, yo' 'osses won't budge when yo' reaches 'em!' Well he found no amount of pulling, pushing, coaxing or swearing moved them an inch, so he went back and said, 'Yo' can 'ave all they bags ont' cart if you'll only mek them 'osses move.' 'No,' she said, 'Jus' one bag to last me the week is all I want.' And sure enough, after he'd delivered the bag, they 'osses moved off without any trouble!

The old school (complete with bell) is now a private house and the Council built a new school on the west side in the 1960s, but this still has strong connections with the church.

The rector has to serve five villages, with three church buildings: the others being Armscote, Blackwell, Darlingscote and Newbold-on-Stour, with about two miles journey between each village. The two busy main roads hinder accessibility.

Blackwell has a population of about 60, with a brick-built village hall and a Methodist chapel. Armscote is a hamlet with approximately 40 residents, has one pub and a Friends' meeting house which holds a meeting once a year. Darlingscote, with a population of less than 60, has a chapel of ease, with a pretty churchyard with cowslips, primroses, daisies and buttercups heralding the spring. It has a club and a cricket club, but the residents now are mostly farmers or weekend cottagers.

🍁 TYSOE

Tysoe is divided into three parts. Approaching from the foot of Sunrising Hill on the A422 Banbury/Stratford road, one comes to Lower Tysoe (known in days gone by as Temple Tysoe, reflecting the fact that lands were held by the Knights Templars of Balsall). Carrying straight on the traveller reaches Middle (or Church) Tysoe, where are clustered the church, inn, village hall, shops, and a fine Methodist church and hall built in 1970. Finally there is Upper (or Over) Tysoe, astride the Shipston/Brailes road. From here one has a view of Tysoe's one remaining windmill, and beyond the windmill lies Compton Wynyates, a great Tudor mansion and the seat of the Marquis of Northampton.

The house, of mellow brick, is prettily sited against wooded hills. The use of brick in 'stone country' is probably due to King Henry VIII's having given the ruined castle of Fulbroke (near Warwick) to Sir William Compton, who in turn salvaged materials and used them at Compton. Unfortunately, this beautiful house is no longer open to the public.

The unusual name of Tysoe actually means 'spur of land dedicated to Tiw', a Germanic god of war, from whom Tuesday takes its name. Around the year AD 600 the conquering Saxons are believed to have cut a huge war horse into the red soil of the hillside, resulting in the area becoming known as the Vale of the Red Horse. The horse-figure seems to have been 'opposite to the East window of Tysoe Church', towards Sunrising Hill. Palm Sunday was the traditional day for annual scouring, but around 1800 the site was ploughed and is now lost for ever under woodland.

William the Conqueror gave Tysoe to one of his followers, Robert de Stafford, and in size and importance it ranked (along with Brailes) next to Warwick. It is a village where the appearance of the fields, with marked 'ridge and furrow' effect, provides clear evidence of the medieval system of open field cultivation. These field patterns are particularly noticeable when the sun is low, or after a light covering of snow.

The church dates from the 11th century, or even earlier, and is dedicated to the Assumption of the Blessed Virgin. There is a Norman doorway, a 14th century octagonal font, a churchyard cross (probably 15th century) and an 18th century bellcote to house a Sanctus bell. The building and contents are lovingly cared for.

The village school takes approximately 150 children from a wide area, covering eight communities.

The lane leading from the churchyard to Peacock Inn is known as Saddledon Street. Local legend describes how, on the eve of the Battle of Edgehill in 1642, a squadron of Royalist cavalry rode through Tysoe, helped themselves to fresh-baked bread, unsaddled their horses in a farmyard and enjoyed a meal of bread, beer and cider! Thoroughly refreshed, they resaddled their horses and went to join King Charles. The lane was thereafter called Saddling Street, and eventually Saddledon Street! A good story anyway.

Next to the post office, in Main Street, is the small Reading Room, bought as a memorial to the men of Tysoe who served in the First World War, and here are their names, proudly recorded in stone. The Second World War Memorial is close by, in front of the police station.

To the right of the War Memorial can be seen a niche which housed a tap for the first piped water supply, and, typical of its period, it bears texts, one being, 'My soul is athirst for God, yea even for the living God', Ps.42.2. Another niche, opposite to the church and at the entrance to the former vicarage, has a seat on either side, presumably for the use of the more elderly or infirm as they waited their turn at the tap, and here there is the text 'Rest in the Lord and wait patiently', Ps.37.7. Did someone have his tongue in cheek?

As a result of the enclosure of the open fields a charitable trust was formed, known as the 'Town Lands', and monies are still distributed.

In the 1880s an Allotments Association was formed, and after much perseverance and many promises of land being found for the project, the Association was eventually able to rent land. This was a tremendous boon to the agricultural workers and others, in very hard times, and the land is still known by the name it was unofficially given during the struggles: 'The Promised Land'.

For over 100 years Tysoe had a valued community fire service, started by the then Marquis of Northampton at Compton Wynyates in 1897 and subsequently based in Tysoe. The service was always manned by volunteer 'retained' firemen pursuing their normal employment but always ready to turn out by day or night, when summoned. For years Tysoe had the distinction of being the only fire station with a thatched roof. Sadly, this had to be abandoned for a purpose-built one when Warwickshire Fire Service supplied a modern appliance which was too high for the old thatched building. Tysoe fire service did of course serve a wide area and was appreciated accordingly by other villages and homes round about. The Brigade had the threat of closure over it for over 20 years and was finally disbanded by Warwickshire County Council and the Home Office on 19th May 1998.

🍁 UFTON

Views from this 380 foot high village extend beyond the ancient Fosse Way and river Avon to the distant Malvern Hills. The name Ufton has undergone many changes since its origin as Ulla's Tun. Ulla was a Danish chief and the word 'tun' means a fortified place.

The remains of early British fortifications can be seen running all round Ufton Hill on which the parish church was built in the 14th century, but a Saxon church stood on the present site as far back as 1042. Beside the gate of the churchyard stands the carved old village cross. At some time its weathered old base disappeared; the cross was buried, and so preserved. It was subsequently discovered in 1862, and, after restoration, placed in its present position. At one time the village was owned by the Spencer family of Althorp Hall.

Formed in 1912, one of the social highlights was a flower show, when eight marquees were hired at a cost of £5 each and as many as 3,000 people attended.

The site of former limestone workings, the Ufton Field Nature Reserve is a Site of Special Scientific Interest. It provides a valuable habitat for aquatic species of insects, some notably rare, a diversity of birds, and has been colonised by plants typical of lime-rich soils, including several species of orchids.

✿ ULLENHALL

The village of Ullenhall, it is believed, was originally built around the 13th century church of St Mark. At the time of the plague the village moved to its present site. The church of St Mark, now known as 'The Old Chapel', was reduced to its present size in 1876.

In 1964 the Hobditch Causeway (a Roman road) was found to run through the garden of Wild Pear Cottage at Dean's Green.

Barrells Hall was built in 1580 and enlarged in 1770. Its most famous resident was Lady Luxborough who was banished there in 1736 by her husband Robert Knight, famous for his family connections with the South Sea Bubble financial disaster. She made the most of her exile and became part of a group of local dilettantes which also included William Somerville of Edstone Hall, William Shenstone of Halesowen and Richard Jago, born in Beaudesert and later of Snitterfield. Since her death Lady

Gentleman's Lane House at Ullenhall

Luxborough is reputed to haunt the ruins. Barrells Hall was badly burnt in 1933.

In 1856 Barrells Hall was purchased by the Newton family. They built St Mary's church and the vicarage in 1875 and the Church of England school and adjacent school house in 1876. The vicarage and land were sold for development in 1973. The school closed in 1987 and in the 1990s the building was converted to a house and three more houses built on the surrounding land.

The village hall was built in 1935 on land given by Mr and Mrs Barber. The hall remains to this day the property of the village and is the centre for village activities.

Over the years the village has had its own post office cum general stores and two other village shops, one combined with an off-licence, but these had all closed by the early 1980s. There has also been a bakery, a blacksmith, a fish and chip shop, a haberdashery, a cafe, a riding school, a boat builder and a garage. All are now past history and the tiny cottages that once housed these businesses have been converted into sought-after modernised cottages. The Winged Spur pub remains popular.

The population of Ullenhall has not altered greatly, being 488 in 1801 and 612 in 1991. Housing varies; there are two small council developments, now partly owner occupied, modern houses and bungalows, and several character houses and cottages.

One of the oldest houses is Hall End Farm which dates from the 17th century and was home to the Booth family. In 1808 John Booth was found in the stable with severe head wounds. His younger brother William, who had a farm at Perry Barr, was charged with his murder. The prosecution alleged that the wounds had been caused by a spade which was covered in blood. However, the defence contested that John had been kicked by a vicious horse. William was acquitted but four years later he was condemned to death after being found guilty of forgery. Unfortunately the rope had not been secured so when the hangman opened the trap Booth fell some ten feet. He was revived but the second time the trap jammed. The hangman succeeded on the third attempt.

One proud boast of Ullenhall is Crowley's Oak – reputed to have been planted over 1,000 years ago.

🍁 WALTON

The tiny village of Walton is a rarity, an excellent example of an estate village, with its buildings still complete, each turning its best face towards the great house, Walton Hall, and its working face to the road. There you can find 15 cottages, plus the old estate office, forge, school house, farm, and the laundry (now renamed Lawnderry House!). The Home Farm, and the Keeper's Cottage are there, together with the Old Rectory, where the present owner, Sir Richard Hamilton, has lived since 1962. His wife, Lady Elizabeth Hamilton has written fascinating books and articles on the history of the Mordaunt family, and the Hall.

There has been some kind of settlement at Walton, on the little river Dene, between the Fosse Way and Wellesbourne, since Iron Age times. The field to the south of the House, the site of the deserted village of Walton d'Eivile, is still known as Old Town.

Walton Hall has not always looked as it does today. It was given a new face in 1862 by the well known Victorian architect and restorer, Gilbert Scott, whose design in the Gothic Revival 'Middle Pointed' style is very reminiscent of 13th and 14th century work. The lake was excavated 13 years later, and in the grounds are a distinctive bridge, known as Gog Bridge, a bath house, and an ice house, as well as the pretty little church of St James, built during the mid-18th century on the site of a previous church.

During this century the Hall has seen many changes. A family home for the widowed Lady Mordaunt for 50 years, it was used by the army during the Second World War (with Lady Mordaunt and her daughter retaining part of it) and was for a time the headquarters of the Free Czechoslovakian Army. Later it was used by the Territorial Army, but when the War Department lease ran out in 1962, it was let to St Vincent's Girls School, and later made into a hotel. Now it is converted to timeshare apartments and brings people from many places to enjoy its rural setting.

One person who knew many happenings in the close knit community was Marjorie Newbery. Her husband Tom was a groom, and in 1926 she started a shop in the front room of their cottage. Here the post box was installed, and daily necessities could be purchased. She retired and closed the shop in 1979, and now the nearest shop is in Wellesbourne. The village school was built in 1831, and by 1860 had 50 children on its roll. Now the few school age children in Walton go daily to Kineton. Post, milk and refuse disposal services come in from outside.

Today the houses are still owned by the estate, but the people who live in them seldom work at Walton Hall. The influence of the Hall is still there. It brings people through the village, cars disturb the utter peace of the valley, but Walton remains wonderfully quiet.

WARMINGTON

Warmington is a small village in the south-east of the county some five or six miles from the market town of Banbury. It is built mainly in the local ironstone, which glows honey-coloured when the sun shines. Like many of the villages in the 'Cotswolds fringe', it has a long history going back way before its first mention in written records in the Conqueror's Domesday Book. Soon after the Norman Conquest, the manor of Warmington was given by the Earl of Warwick to the Abbey of Preaux in Normandy and a small priory was built in Warmington. Although the priory has long since gone, its influence lives on in the architecture of the parish church and perhaps in the planned layout of the village around a large green.

Attractive houses border the green and these include the Manor House, dating from the 1580s, and the former rectory whose Georgian front conceals its earlier origins. The green today is used mainly for recreation. There are informal sports, an annual fete, 5th November bonfire and, on Christmas Eve, carol-singing around a tree which is lit for the twelve days of Christmas. Ducks still spend their day on the green and splash in the pool. Until the 1960s the green was grazed by cows, horses and geese, and until the 1930s the washbrook below the pool was where the annual sheepwashing took place. Flocks were brought in from all the neighbouring parishes to be penned on the green, together with the sheep of the parish, awaiting their turn to be washed.

Tradition tells us that villagers wanted to build their church upon the green but that fairies came by night and repeatedly stole the stones away to the hill-top site where the church stands in splendid isolation upon a rocky outcrop. The church is dedicated to St Michael, a favourite dedication for a hill-top church. Inside the church, above a former chapel which is now the vestry, there is an upper room which at one time was the home of a priest. This is the oldest 'house' in the parish, complete with all mod cons – a fireplace, garderobe (lavatory) and extensive views! Today's rector, with four parishes to serve, finds his 1960s house in the village rather more commodious!

In the churchyard are no fewer than 80 listed gravestones, testifying to the skills of local masons. One memorial commemorates Alexander Gourdin, a Royalist Captain who fell at the battle of Edgehill, which was fought just over the parish boundary. The rector of the day, meanwhile, had deserted his flock to captain a troop for the Parliamentarians.

From the 17th century onwards, village homes were rebuilt and extended as the fortunes of Warmington yeomen and smallholders improved. Some of their homes carry datestones or have dated beams. Many smallholders combined farming with trades such as weaving, shoemaking, baking, stone cutting and building. Modern renovators occasionally find good luck tokens placed in their homes by earlier owners – old shoes and buckles in inglenooks, stone bottles in the roofs and sheep bells in barn walls.

During the 19th century, when population was rapidly increasing and work could be hard to come by, village life became insupportable for many families. Sons and daughters left Warmington to seek their fortunes in towns, cities and the colonies. Many who stayed found comfort in Methodism. Both Wesleyans and Primitives had their adherents. The present chapel, dated 1811, is one of the oldest in the Banbury circuit. Prudent folk flocked to join a Court of the Ancient Order of Foresters, to provide against sickness and old age. Their Foresters' Hall still remains, though put to other use. The present allotments serve to remind of the time when three sets of allotments around the village helped to eke out family budgets. Many tiny cottages, with thatched roofs and earth floors, were abandoned at that time, although their ruins around the higher parts of the village were still visible within living memory.

A few new homes have been built in recent years, mostly on lower ground, continuing the gradual drift down the hillside. Barns are converted for residential use; no new phenomenon, for in 1635 Quarter Sessions record permission for a Warmington barn conversion! A few of the old village families remain and farming continues. Most villagers now are commuters although a significant number work from home, recalling the weavers, shoemakers and masons of yesteryear. Two doors up from the Plough inn stands the Old School, closed in 1970, and bought by the village in 1995 to provide an improved village hall. This houses not only the playgroup – itself a bit of village history having an unbroken 30 year existence – but also many other social and educational activities. Some activities fill a need for a time and then fade. Others like Whist and the WI go on for ever!

🍁 WARTON

A mystery surrounds the very name of the village of Warton! No mention of Warton is found in the Domesday Book (1086), though the nearby village of Orton-on-the-Hill is chronicled under the name of Wartone, leading many students of local history to believe that Warton, as it is at present, did not exist at that time, a view that is borne out by the fact that only one medieval building, with a very small part of another, exists in Warton to this day.

It is probable that the present Warton was part of the estate of the owner of the land at Orton, and that the windmill for grinding corn which may well have existed at Warton at that time (there was a windmill here until recent times) was also within the demesne of the then Lord of the Manor of 'Wartone'. It may also be significant that the oldest public house, The Fox and Dogs, is at Little Warton (once a hamlet in its own right, though now an integral part of Warton village). The other two, the Boot Inn, and The Hatter's Arms are of relatively recent origin.

The agricultural land surrounding the present village has always been noted for its great productivity, owing much to the fact that in the Middle Ages it was entirely under water for most of the winter and spring. The annual floods bring with them a highly fertile silt-marl, in which farmers, allotment-holders, and gardeners come across the typical rounded pebbles of a river valley. It is possible that only the advent of coalmining in the early years of the 19th century led to the land being readily available for cultivation, as it may have been the many shallow mines that caused the unforeseen drainage of the area!

Housing now occupies many former farm sites. These farms – Ivycroft, Windmill, Cope's, Hill Crest and Willis's – were the last examples of an old system where the farmhouse fronted the main street in the village. Thirty five years ago the majority of the farms in Warton had their house fronting the main street. Hill Crest Farm, now renamed Willows Farm has moved to the outskirts of the village surrounded by its fields, which is how most of us today perceive farms. Houses were built on the land previously occupied by Ivycroft, Cope's, Hill Crest and Willis's farms and Windmill Farm was razed to the ground to be replaced by a new First school. The actual farmhouses at Willis's and Hill Crest farms still remain. Members of the Willis family had farmed in Warton for almost 100 years.

As in many villages all over England there is the ubiquitous apochryphal legend of the 'pig on the wall, watching the band go by', which may in Warton's case have an element of truth – pigs are still bred and reared here.

The present Holy Trinity (Church of England) church at

Warton dates only from the middle of the 19th century and there is no evidence of a previous church on the site, or even in the village, though at one time there were no less than three non-conformist chapels. These were probably erected as a result of Warton's becoming a village inhabited by miners, though there was no mine in Warton itself.

That there was little if any proper sanitation in the miners' two-up-and-two-down cottages is borne out by evidence that soon after the church was built, a significantly large number of whole families were buried within the space of a few years. This was during the cholera epidemic of 1850–60. A row of gravestones bearing the same surname, Hull, and the ages ranging from a few months to 45 years or so, is a sad reminder of those times.

Most of the inhabitants work in nearby towns and cities, principally Birmingham, Tamworth and Leicester. Though at one time it was possible to purchase virtually all one's household requirements in the village – there was a butcher, a baker, a shoemaker, a blacksmith, a garage and petrol station, a tailor, a general store – these have disappeared one by one, leaving only two general stores, one of which is also a post office.

The earliest school in the village was opened in 1832, and was held in the schoolmaster's house, which still exists, though it is now a private dwelling-house. Behind it is the old village school, built about the time of the Education Act 1870, now used by the Playschool and various village groups including the WI. The First School built in 1975 on the former Windmill Farm site became a Primary School in 1994.

🍁 WATER ORTON

The village of Water Orton has grown steadily through the years, its early name being 'Overton', meaning 'a settlement upon the river bank'. This area of high land lies either side of Old Church Road on the south side of the river Tame.

Two half-timbered buildings, known as The Chestnuts, circa

15th century, and Wakefield House, circa 16th century, can still be seen on the southern edge of the old village. To the north of these properties is the now abandoned graveyard. Once within its walls stood the first church buildings. Early records show that a Chapel of Ease was here in 1347. This attractive title meant that the chapel was a more convenient place for the villagers to worship in, rather than travelling all the way to Aston, where the 'mother' church could be found. For many years, Water Orton belonged to the huge parish of Aston, then in August 1871 it was formed into an ecclesiastical parish.

The base and shaft of an ancient stone cross can still be seen in the old graveyard. This edifice has survived the chapel and was once the open air pulpit used by the travelling preachers of long ago to spread the gospel to the settlers.

Many pottery shards dug up from the garden of Wakefield House some years ago were dated as early as the 13th century. Some are possibly of Roman origin, making Overton a place with a very long history. The word 'Water' first appears in documents of the 16th century and today, after the slightest shower, it can be seen why it was added!

Almost a quarter of a mile to the south lies the village green, another interesting area. At its eastern corner once stood an old cottage, demolished in 1951. Records dated it back to the 13th century and, with solid (brick) upper floors, it may have been a malt house, which would have been used for storing barley grain ready for the making of ale. Another feature of the cottage was a huge baking oven and deep garden well. The village school overlooks the green from the south and was built during 1878. Several modern extensions have made it into a large educational centre.

The village has two public houses, The Digby Hotel built about 1860 and The Dog (1722). Two others, both of which could be found in the Coleshill Road, have long since disappeared, their sites now occupied by new buildings.

It was, of course, the railway that assured the village of a future. Until 1842 this was just a scattering of little cottages and farms. Water Orton station brought in visitors and new residents by the score. In no time at all a small farming settlement had become a busy little village. Many large gentlemen's residences were built; all, alas, no longer standing; their sites now containing flats, a clinic, houses, a Methodist chapel, maisonettes and a road. A large and very busy railway siding to the west of the village offered many jobs to Water Orton during the steam era. It was always said that if you worked on the railway you were well off!

Today employment can be found on the huge industrial estate only a mile away near Coleshill, or a few hundred yards over the old 'Vesey' river bridge at the growing factory by the river Tame. This large complex produces many goods made of UPVC, including the fast expanding trade of window frames.

The railway station sees much activity as does the 109 year old church, sadly now without its spire. The Methodist chapel (1868) is well attended and there is also the Catholic church hall of St John the Baptist (1966).

With the M6 relief road, Water Orton will be completely surrounded by motorways, securing its future as a village forever!

🍁 WEETHLEY

Weethley comes from an Anglo-Saxon word meaning withy clearing or withywood, and is mentioned in the Domesday Book of 1086. It is situated approximately three miles from Alcester along the Ridgeway, between Redditch and Evesham. It has always been a small place, although from the contours of the land it is presumed there were more dwellings in the vicinity at one time. Some of the cottages are 17th century timber framed, although most of them have now been renovated and brought in line with today's building regulations, while still retaining their old world charm. At one time all the land belonged to the Marquis of Hertford who owns Ragley Hall.

The church of St James was rebuilt in late 13th century style in 1857, and is located on a hillside, which is the highest point in the area and has beautiful views of the Cotswolds from the porch. Just outside the gate is a pond. This tiny church holds a congregation of approximately 100. A service is held at the church every Sunday and, according to records, has been held without interruption since before 1900. Unfortunately, this record was broken in 1967 by the outbreak of Foot and Mouth Disease which threatened the churchwarden's stock. Although his farm was spared the church was inaccessible for six weeks.

Each year on the 1st May more than 20 Morris dancers and musicians and about 60 onlookers gather on the hillside by the church to revive a centuries-old ceremony to greet the dawn of the first day of May. The White Hart Morris Men, who are based at Redditch, revived the ancient tradition in 1980. They dance for almost an hour, gather in the church for coffee and then adjourn to The Swan Inn in Alcester.

Although Weethley is only a very small place it has a lot to offer: peace, tranquillity, the beauty of the changing seasons and, of course, the wildlife – the birds, the rabbits and the deer. There have been very few changes during the last century and it is to be hoped that during the next century Weethley will remain much the same.

WELFORD-ON-AVON & WESTON-ON-AVON

Along the river Avon, approximately five miles westward from Stratford, are the villages of Weston and Welford-on-Avon. These two villages consist of timbered, thatched, black and white cottages, typical of Shakespeare country, with Victorian and modern properties scattered in between.

Welford was originally established in Saxon times by monks from Deerhurst in Gloucestershire and is the larger village of the two. Weston is a small cluster of houses and a church, nearby. Over the centuries most of the villagers were small holders, self sufficient, and not beholden to a Lord of the Manor. Local trades recorded were farmworkers, shoemakers, spinners, cider makers, needle polishers, glove makers and blacksmiths.

The original Saxon church in Welford was built by the Priory of Deerhurst. The church, as seen today, is Perpendicular style, on Norman foundations. In the church is a Saxon font bowl, and a carved wooden screen dedicated to the 'Fallen of the First World War'.

Weston church was built in the 15th century in Perpendicular style by John Greville of nearby Milcote Manor. Joseph Green, vicar of Weston in 1735 was an influential public figure in Stratford and discovered and copied William Shakespeare's will – a copy of which is in the British Museum.

On the village green in Welford is a maypole, 65 feet tall – one of only five in the country. It is known to have existed in the 14th century. The original wooden maypole was struck by lightning and blown down, and was replaced with a metal one with a running fox weathervane. It is painted, red, white and blue stripe, every 10 years. Village schoolchildren dance around the maypole annually in July.

Over the centuries tales have emerged of characters living in Welford & Weston. There is the 'Wicked Loddy' – the bogey man the children lived in fear of. The son of Sir Edward Greville of Milcote Manor, he was the notorious Lodvic Greville who was pressed to death with stones in 1589 for murder.

Welford & Weston is a busy thriving community today. Welford has a population of approximately 1,500. It has a post office, village stores, butcher, school, church and three pubs, and has won the Warwickshire Best Kept Village competition.

Tourism is the main industry providing employment in Stratford and the Cotswolds for the locals and new cottage industries have evolved in the village itself.

🍁 WELLESBOURNE

Wellesbourne lies within 10 miles of Stratford, Warwick, Leamington and Kineton – a large village which, although not notably pretty, has attractive quiet corners and a charm that increases upon closer inspection. It seems initially a village without a centre and maps often show two names, Wellesbourne

Mountford and Wellesbourne Hastings. The two Wellesbournes take their names from local families, no longer remembered as often as they were, for the village is now known to all but cartographers simply as Wellesbourne.

Lying to the north, Wellesbourne Hastings had at its heart the church of St Peter, with its 15th century tower, set in a pleasant little side road between the Old Vicarage, the Malt House, and The King's Head. This hostelry, despite modern additions on the northern aspect, still gives a rural feeling to the end of Church Street, where some of the older houses stand, and where there was once a charter for an annual fair.

Wellesbourne Mountford was the southern part of the modern village, centred around the picturesque Chestnut Square, with a distinctive thatched pub, The Stag's Head, in one corner. It was in Chestnut Square that Joseph Arch, in 1872, inaugurated the first trade union for agricultural workers, an event which is still commemorated with an annual parade, and marked by an unusual memorial – a plaque in the bus shelter. The buildings in Church Walk and Chapel Street are very much as he would have known them.

Further south than Chestnut Square is the sports field, with regular matches of bowls, football and hockey, as well as cricket on a green which boasts of being among the oldest in Britain, and was mentioned in *Tom Brown's Schooldays*.

During the Second World War farmland to the south-west of the main village was requisitioned as an airfield and used by the RAF and the Canadian airforce. Following this, the airfield was used for occasional flying and then developed as a small aerodrome for light aircraft. The old Dovehouse Farm, the domestic site, was not suitable for return to its former use and was finally used for housing in the 1980s. Local names, and those of the aircraft that flew from the aerodrome, have been preserved in the street names.

The two halves merge at the river Dene, a shallow river, once prone to high floods, which meets the Avon in Charlecote. It is crossed by a two lane bridge, which marks both the centre of the village and the link between its two wards. The separate Parish

Councils were amalgamated in 1947, and the amalgamated Council also covers Walton, an old estate village lying in seclusion 1½ miles to the south-east.

Just by the bridge is Dog Close, its name connecting it with The Talbot, just across the road. It was here the landlord originally grew the ingredients for the beer. Mostly now it is used for grazing, but the occasional village carnival takes place where once the ground was levelled to accommodate the tug of war teams. Today's residents regard the field as the 'green lung' of Wellesbourne and preserve the open space as part of a conservation area.

Although not strictly within the boundaries of the village, Wellesbourne is known internationally because of the National Vegetable Research Station, now part of Horticulture Research International, which uses much of the open farmland to the west of the village. Here scientists work on problems connected with the breeding and raising of vegetables, and have given many new varieties to the grower, as well as preserving historic ones in a special gene bank.

Recent additions to Wellesbourne have greatly increased the population, starting with several developments in the 1960s and followed in the 1980s by the 800 houses on the Dovehouse estate. Despite this, Wellesbourne is still proud to call itself a village, and retains the feel of a village.

🍁 WHATCOTE

Whatcote is small and peaceful, lying between Oxhill and Idlicote, but small or not, it is recorded in the Domesday Book.

The Royal Oak is 17th century and a very popular venue. Farms, houses and bungalows cluster round the ancient parish church of St Peter and the little Methodist church built in 1905.

It is interesting to look at St Peter's, surrounded by fields, (on a site which has seen a church for nearly 1,000 years) and to realise that the present building yet managed to get itself hit by a stray enemy bomb at the time of the Coventry blitz in late 1940! An old font, which is Norman or even earlier, was damaged by the

German bomb, but has been skilfully repaired.

Marks on the east wall of the tower exterior show clearly how the pitch of the roof has been altered at some time, and one can also see, carved into the tower battlements, an inverted chevron on a shield – the coat-of-arms of the Earls of Stafford. The Staffords were Lords of the Manor until about 1520 when the village was sold to the Northamptons. The shaft of the old preaching cross is medieval, but is now mounted on an octagonal base, probably 18th century.

❧ WILLOUGHBY

Willoughby is a village on the very edge of Warwickshire. The border with Northamptonshire is only a few yards along the A45 on the way to Daventry. Consequently, it may not be known to many people outside its own area. However, one way of introducing the village is by a question. What have Willoughby and Lilliput in common? The answer is not just that both are small places but something much more interesting. The answer is Dean Swift, Jonathan Swift of *Gulliver's Travels*.

The story is told in Willoughby that Dean Swift used to travel from London to Holyhead by road, en route for Ireland. He would sometimes spend a night at The Three Crosses Inn at Willoughby in order to break his journey. Jonathan Swift was an arrogant and irascible character but he apparently met his match in the landlady of The Three Crosses. On one occasion she so angered him that he wrote with his diamond ring on the window pane for the attention of the landlord

> You have three crosses
> On your door
> Hang up your wife
> And she'll make four.

Thereafter the inn became known as the Four Crosses and there are four crosses on the wall of the present building which has now been converted into private flats.

Willoughby is a pleasant place to live. It is far enough from any large town for it to preserve a sense of rural peace. But large centres like Coventry, Northampton and Leamington Spa are all easily accessible in this age of the motor car. Most people work outside the village although a number operate small businesses from their homes.

Cricket has been played in Willoughby for over a hundred years but the present club was founded in 1901. This club has a good local reputation for excellence of cricket and club spirit and it attracts players, social members and spectators from quite a wide area.

This is an ancient village, being mentioned in the Domesday Book and the records of Magdalen College which go back to the 15th century. Vale House and The Rose Inn are probably the oldest dwellings. The inn is at least 400 years old.

The church is very ancient indeed. There is a record of its existence in 1215 although, of course, parts of the building were added at different times. The lychgate, which looks old, was built in 1977 to commemorate the Queen's Silver Jubilee. It is built of weathered stone to harmonise with the church. A very interesting feature of the church is the carillon or turret clock. This was brought from Southam in 1724. It was out of use for nearly 50 years but was restored to working order in 1983. Most of the cost was subscribed by the Willoughby Foundation, which forms part of the ancient and munificent Willoughby Charities. Five well known tunes can be played upon the carillon.

The Willoughby Charities were established by John Hayward and his wife Margaret in 1437. John Brook, another benefactor is recorded as having made his charitable bequest in 1535, during the reign of Henry VIII. John is remembered in the name of Brooks Close which was a field adjoining the churchyard. It is now an attractive curve of bungalows built in the 1960s but still carrying the name of Brooks Close.

The name Willoughby was probably better known when the main LNER line passed through Braunston and Willoughby Station. Line and station are no longer to be seen so we are left with just the name Willoughby, said to be derived from Willowbec because of the willow trees that still grow beside the little brook which flows along by the village street.

The brook has for many years been prone to flooding, causing damage to properties and inconvenience to villagers. Many residents born and bred in Willoughby maintain the Oxford Canal was the problem. Having no concrete evidence, British Waterways would not accept responsibility. However, the Easter floods of 1998 brought a new dimension to the flooding of Willoughby. Video footage showed a massive intake of water in a short space of time, highlighting without a doubt where the problem lay. British Waterways have now spent a considerable amount of money on piling banks, and maintaining proper usage of sluice systems. It is with a promise of more monitoring of the canal in the future, that Willoughby looks forward to a drier century.

🍁 WILMCOTE

Wilmcote is three miles north of Stratford-upon-Avon, with a population of about 1,200. It is mainly a dormitory settlement but with mixed farming taking place and some small businesses located within the village.

Wilmcote developed during the 19th century due to the quarries and close proximity to the newly built canal and railway transport system. At that time over half the population worked at the local quarries producing high quality floor stone and marble known as blue lias, some of which was used at the Palace of Westminster in London. The village also contained extensive fruit orchards supplying local markets. These survived until the mid 20th century.

There were five public houses serving this small community. Now there are just two, the Masons Arms and the Mary Arden Inn.

The gem in the heart of Wilmcote is of course Mary Arden's House, the childhood home of Shakespeare's mother. It is a beautiful half-timbered house of the 16th century. It was once a hall house and would have looked rather different in those days. Bedrooms have been added at a later date, the thatched roof replaced by handmade tiles and a stone floor laid. Originally, the house would have had a solar, a room for sleeping, over the kitchen for the use of the family. Servants and workers would have slept on the floor around the fire in the centre of the room, the smoke finding its way out through a hole in the thatch. It would have had an earth floor with rushes scattered upon it.

As the winter wore on more rushes were added, building up into a sort of compost heap, full of vermin. When springtime came around (and the floor was high in more senses than one!), it was time for spring cleaning. The rotting rushes would be thrown onto the midden outside the back door. The interior of the house would be white-washed, including the beams. It is a fairly modern idea to leave the beams unwhitewashed.

Today the house is open to the public and furnished with some

St Andrew's Church, Wilmcote

lovely old oak pieces. There is an old board table, a hutch cupboard and a monk's bench made about 1480. It is a farmhouse and the farm buildings are full of things of interest, artefacts and farm implements collected over many years.

One of the best of the buildings is the dovecote. As Robert Arden was the lord of the manor he was the only man in the village with a dovecote. It has over 600 pigeon holes and at nesting time would house about 3,000 birds. (With a bit of luck his pigeons would have fed on his neighbours' land, come home to roost in his dovecote and ended up on his table!)

Mary was the youngest of Robert Arden's eight daughters. Having no sons when he died, his only unmarried daughter living at home, Mary, inherited her father's property.

John Shakespeare, hearing of this heiress at Wilmcote came hotfoot from Stratford to court her. They were married and he carried her off to Stratford where he was in business as a glover and leather worker. William was their eldest son.

The house remained in the family, being occupied for a while by Mary's sister who was married to a man called Edkins. There are still people called Edkins living in the area.

Most of the estate has long since broken up but the house, buildings and the Glebe farmhouse next door are now owned by the Shakespeare Birthplace Trust and open throughout the year as a museum attracting visitors from all over the world.

Wilmcote is one of the few small villages to retain its railway station and still has a regular service from Stratford.

Alongside the railway runs the Stratford Canal, built in the early 1800s to carry the limestone from the quarry and up to 500,000 tons of coal a year from the Midland coal fields. Until recently the stretch of canal from Stratford to Wilmcote was in the care of the National Trust but has been taken over by British Waterways. After years of neglect it is now carrying many holiday boats on the way to Stratford to join the river.

❧ WISHAW

Wishaw is almost part of Sutton Coldfield, and was mentioned in the Domesday Survey of 1086 when it was known as Witscaga, meaning 'mountain ash by the curving hollow'. The present population is under 200, less than that recorded in the Domesday Survey.

From Edward the Confessor's time Wishaw and nearby Moxhull had been manors of the Knights Templars, and in 1257 Wishaw was granted to Walter de Beresford, whose descendants were still living in the parish in the 20th century. They are commemorated in Wishaw church, dedicated to St Chad, Bishop of Lichfield from 669 to 672. Built on the site of an old Roman church, originally it would have been constructed of timber, but the earliest part of the present building dates back to the 13th century with later additions from the 15th to 19th centuries. One interesting feature of the church is a hagioscope, or 'leper's squint'. From here, lepers would be able to see the altar from outside the church and watch the preparation and administration of the sacrament. The church bells would also ring the curfew for the charcoal burners of the Forest of Arden, of which this area was once part.

The church also has a memorial to Thomas Baylis, the village schoolmaster for 31 years, who 'amassed a plentiful fortune' and in 1744 donated several gifts of money to the church and the poor of the parish and '10 shillings a year for one scholar's expenses at the school'. The school, now Church Farm, was a few yards from the church.

The old Cock Inn, a well-known local landmark, has been enlarged and modernised in recent years and was reputedly one of Dick Turpin's hiding places. There were two other coaching inns in the village, both on the former London Road (now the main A446): The Mother Redcap Inn and The Green Man. Both are still standing but have been private houses for many years.

The Memorial Hall was built by public subscription in 1923 to honour the fallen of the First World War. Almost next door are the former workhouses, now two pretty cottages.

216

One of the oldest buildings in Wishaw, and indeed in the whole of Sutton Coldfield, is The Grove, which has unusual cruck trusses (a type of oak beam) naturally curved to form an arch which support the walls and roof. Other interesting buildings in the village are located in Wiggins Hill Road: the Old Barn, a black and white half-timbered cottage and barn; Wiggins Hill Farm which has an unusual curved Dutch gable; and Quaker Cottage, formerly a Quaker Meeting House built in 1724 which served the many Quakers living in the area at that time. Now a private house, a Quaker burial ground is reputedly situated near the garden wall.

The well-known Belfry Hotel, Golf and Leisure Centre is on the site of Old Moxhull Hall. This was once the home of one of the district's most prominent families, the Rylands, but was destroyed by the family earlier in the 20th century as there was a superstition that it was responsible for the deaths of several family members. New Moxhull Hall was built nearby, and is now also a hotel.

The Belfry is now the home of the Professional Golfers'Association and its Brabazon Course has been made famous in recent years as home to several Ryder Cup matches.

Nowadays, Wishaw has no school, village shop, or even a bus service, but it is still a thriving community. The majority of the village lies within the Green Belt and is still largely agricultural. Unlike its near neighbours Middleton, Curdworth and Minworth, Wishaw has not seen any new housing development in recent years, but it sadly lives under the threat of the encroaching Midlands motorway network.

🍁 WOLVEY

The village of Wolvey lies almost on the boundary between Warwickshire and Leicestershire. To the north-east of the village runs Watling Street, now the A5, and just across the parish boundary to the south is the Fosse Way. Because of this unique crossing point between two major ancient highways Wolvey has always been a village of transit, a stopping place for travellers rather than a centre of more stable activities. This pattern must have developed centuries ago. Abbey Farm, just to the north of Wolvey has a neolithic barrow on its lands and the largest scatter of flints anywhere in Warwickshire.

The proximity of the two great roads meant that great armies must have passed close by or even through the village. In 1469 Edward IV fought a battle on Wolvey Heath, was defeated and captured by Warwick the Kingmaker, and taken on to imprisonment in Middleham Castle, in Yorkshire, home of the legendary Richard III. But extant records also include happier occasions, such as the welcoming of Queen Elizabeth I 'with a great company of nobles' in the centre of the village by the Mayor of the City of Coventry and his colleagues 'in skarlett gownes with foot clothes' in 1566, as she progressed from Leicester and crossed the county boundary.

Like so many Warwickshire villages, Wolvey today is a mixture of architectural styles from different periods and its small population includes descendants of earlier inhabitants besides many newcomers attracted by the bracing winds that once made Wolvey famous for its proliferation of windmills (now, alas, all vanished), its lush farmland and its pedigree. For Wolvey, as the name indicates, was once a Saxon settlement and the name may mean 'enclosure to protect flocks from wolves', proving that when the Forest of Arden stretched across the county, Wolvey offered a haven, a place of respite in the wilderness. The first mention of Wolvey (Ulvetha) in the Domesday Book of 1086 notes that there were 15 villagers and one priest.

The most mysterious and most poignant story from Wolvey's past is the strange case of Lady Dorothy Smythe who, as Dugdale claims in his *Antiquities of Warwickshire*, published in 1656 'was burnt at a Stake near the Hermitage on Wolvey heath (towards the side of Shirford lordship) where the country people to this day shew the place'. Dugdale's 'Shirford' was, in fact, Shelford, a manor just outside the boundary of Wolvey and of which nothing remains today except the name, which belongs to one of the local farms. Lady Dorothy, married to Sir Walter Smythe, had been mistress of Shelford until her death in 1555. Her brutal death was in consequence of being found guilty of her husband's murder two years earlier.

Changes inevitably take place in the village as the years go by. Wolvey is now a commuter village with easy access to many parts of the country with the M69, M1 and M6 motorways passing close by. 'Shanks's pony' of olden days has been replaced by cycles and cars, while in farming 'horse power' has changed from animal to mechanical.

The old school has closed and a larger new one replaces it; only one shop remains from the range of trades and the bakeries we once had; and there is no policeman living in the village today. The firm of Galliford's, known countrywide, started in the village with one road roller and now huge machinery takes its place.

The Anglican and Catholic churches, with the chapel, meet the spiritual needs of the community. The village hall is a meeting place for clubs and societies, and a venue for many activities. Leisure time is catered for with the playing field for football, cricket and tennis and the green for bowls in the summer – and fishing lakes abound.

🍁 WOOTTON WAWEN

Despite its postal address, which would have the unwary believe it is part of the suburban sprawl of the West Midlands, Wootton Wawen has its roots secure in the soil of Warwickshire. To this day the village owes its allegiance to that county – whatever the post office might say.

Wootton Wawen has strong claims to being one of the oldest villages in Warwickshire. The village takes its name from the Saxon words 'wudu', meaning wood, and 'tun', an enclosed piece of land. The suffix Wawen was introduced to distinguish it from other Warwickshire Woottons and comes from Wagen, the Saxon thane who held the land immediately prior to the Norman Conquest.

Wootton Wawen was recorded in the Domesday Book, when St

Peter's church stood where it does today. The church still retains its Saxon tower and is set in an immaculate churchyard which won the Diocesan 'Best Kept' competition in 1998.

Next to the church stands Wootton Hall, a handsome Italianate stone construction dating from 1637. Until recent times the Hall was owned by Catholic families (principally the Caringtons) and numerous stories and legends have been woven through its history. Mrs Fitzherbert, the morganatic wife of King George IV, spent her childhood at the Hall and visited it after her marriage. The hauntingly perfumed ghost of the Grey Lady, who wanders the Hall, is said to be her.

The Mill, now converted into homes, has played a vital role in the life of the village. In addition to making paper, grinding corn, and generating the Hall's electricity, it was the social centre until the building of the first village hall in 1946.

The former Catholic school adjoins the Mill and, on the Henley side of Wootton is the old village Board school. Both are now converted into private homes and children attend the modern county primary school.

Opposite the Mill is the attractive pink-washed Priory and, as

The Stratford Canal at Wootton Wawen Basin

one drives through the village to Birmingham, there are many picturesque black and white timbered buildings, notably The Bull's Head Inn, the Old Vicarage, and Manor Farm with its unusual and attractive carved plaster door canopy.

Leaving the village on the Stratford side one passes Austy Manor, once a private home and now the headquarters of the British Pregnancy Advisory Service. The Fieldhouse family from Austy endowed the Seymour Homes in memory of their son in Sri Lanka. The homes provide accommodation for elderly residents.

Further out on the edge of the parish boundary is the reconstructed Edstone Hall. It was once the ancestral home of the Somerville family. The poet William Somerville wrote his acclaimed work *The Chase*, while living here. More recently Edstone was a nature cure centre. It is now used commercially.

Tucked away behind the village shop is Little Croft, once the village workhouse. Along the public footpath across the fields are Blue Hole Cottages, ancient cruck-framed buildings painstakingly restored.

In the past Wootton was principally an agricultural community, with the majority of the population employed on the farms and large estates. A thriving hurdle-making industry was centred on the osier beds.

Although the village has grown it still supports many flourishing farms, a market garden, three garages, two pubs, a retail caravan outlet, canal boat hire business, and a number of successful 'cottage' industries, at Yew Tree Farm Craft Centre.

Transport has had a great influence over the life of the village. The A3400 trunk road cuts a swathe through its centre and a 1960s road-widening scheme deprived Wootton of its Parson's Pond and tree-lined verge. The Stratford Canal, constructed in the late 18th century, is carried in spectacular manner over the A3400 by an aqueduct built in 1813. The Stratford to Birmingham railway line also provides Wootton with a vital transport link. In the past special trains brought keen anglers in pursuit of their sport, and huge crowds from Birmingham to enjoy the annual flower show.

🍁 INDEX